# World War II: Essential Histories

# World War II:

The Mediterranean 1940–1945

Robert O'Neill, Series Editor; and Paul Collier

ROSEN
PUBLISHING

New York

This edition published in 2010 by:

The Rosen Publishing Group, Inc.
29 East 21st Street
New York, NY 10010

Additional end matter copyright © 2010 by The Rosen Publishing Group, Inc.

## Library of Congress Cataloging-in-Publication Data

Collier, Paul H. (Paul Henry).
World War II: The Mediterranean, 1940–1945 / Paul Collier.
   p. cm.—(World War II: Essential histories)
"Robert O'Neill, series editor."
Originally published as v. 4 in The Second World War. Oxford : Osprey, 2002–2003.
Includes bibliographical references and index.
ISBN 978-1-4358-9132-6 (library binding)
1. World War, 1939–1945—Campaigns—Mediterranean Region—Juvenile literature. I. O'Neill,
Robert John. II. Second World War. III. Title. IV. Title: World War Two.
D763.M47C656 2010
940.54'293—dc22

                                                                          2009031245

*Manufactured in Malaysia*

CPSIA Compliance Information: Batch #TW10YA: For Further Information contact Rosen Publishing, New York, New York at 1-800-237-9932

**On the cover:** Armored vehicles in desert, 1940 *(Australian War Memorial).*

# Contents

Introduction 5

Chronology 8

Background to war
Italian imperialism 10

Warring sides
Italian propaganda, German professionalism,
and Allied industrialization 15

Outbreak
A parallel war 22

The fighting
In all directions at once 27

Portrait of a soldier
A modest hero 59

The world around war
Politics and war 64

Portrait of a civilian
A child in the siege of annihilation: Malta 1940–43 73

How the war ended
Not necessarily in peace 77

Conclusions and consequences
The end of empire 80

Glossary 89

For More Information 90

For Further Reading 91

Bibliography 91

Index 94

# Introduction

Confrontation in the Mediterranean region between the Western Allies and the Axis powers began seven months before Adolf Hitler occupied the Rhineland and ended only after his suicide in a Berlin bunker in May 1945. The repercussions of this epic struggle continued for many years, however, and still maintain the world's attention.

The road to war in Europe took an irrevocable turn when Benito Mussolini invaded Ethiopia in October 1935. For the first time the old world powers and the international authority of the League of Nations succumbed to the aggressive ambition of the dictators and their fascist regimes. Mussolini was determined to redress the sense of national impotence that ensued from the settlement of the First World War, in which many Italians believed that Italy failed to receive the rewards due to a victor, by building a new Roman empire in the Mediterranean and assuming the status of a first-rate power from a position of strength.

Although the sun was setting on her empire, Britain retained a vital interest in the Mediterranean. The Suez Canal, which Anthony Eden called the "windpipe" of the empire, cut about 3,500 miles (5,600 km) or

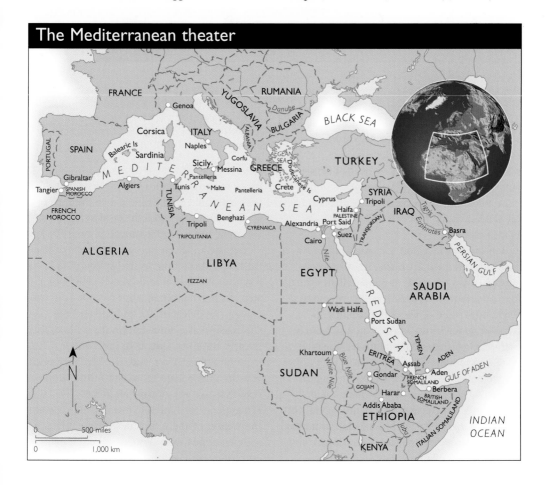

## The Mediterranean theater

FRANCE
Genoa
RUMANIA
Danube
BLACK SEA
Corsica
ITALY
YUGOSLAVIA
BULGARIA
ALBANIA
Naples
SPAIN
Balearic Is
Sardinia
Corfu
AEGEAN SEA
TURKEY
PORTUGAL
M E D I T E R
Sicily
Messina
GREECE
Dodecanese Is
Gibraltar
Pantelleria
Tangier
SPANISH MOROCCO
Algiers
Tunis
Malta
Pantelleria
Crete
Cyprus
SYRIA
Tripoli
IRAQ
FRENCH MOROCCO
TUNISIA
A N E A N   S E A
Haifa
PALESTINE
TRANSJORDAN
Tigris
Tripoli
Benghazi
Alexandria
Port Said
Euphrates
Basra
TRIPOLITANIA
CYRENAICA
Cairo
Suez
ALGERIA
LIBYA
Nile
EGYPT
PERSIAN GULF
FEZZAN
SAUDI ARABIA
Wadi Halfa
Port Sudan
RED SEA
N
Khartoum
White Nile
Blue Nile
ERITREA
Assab
YEMEN
ADEN
GULF OF ADEN
SUDAN
Gondar
FRENCH SOMALILAND
Aden
GOJJAM
Berbera
Harar
BRITISH SOMALILAND
Addis Ababa
ETHIOPIA
INDIAN OCEAN
ITALIAN SOMALILAND
Juba
0    500 miles
0    1,000 km
KENYA

almost one-third off the passage to the East. Through this vital artery flowed her commerce, her administrators and her military and, with a growing dependence on Middle Eastern oil, the waterway gained a new significance. With naval bases at the colonial outposts of Gibraltar, Malta, and Alexandria, Britain dominated the Mediterranean region, the strategic importance of which was immeasurable.

Tension in the region remained high as both sides used the Spanish Civil War as an effective dress rehearsal to prepare their armed forces. Moreover, this prelude also encouraged the natural coalescence of the Italian and German regimes into a fascist bloc, although each retained their own ambitions. Together France and Britain dominated the Mediterranean region, and when war erupted in September 1939, Italy was in such a poor state of military preparation, despite 20 years of boasts to the contrary by Mussolini, that it was forced to remain neutral. The fall of France and the imminent collapse of Britain, however,

presented an opportunity that Mussolini believed would enable him to reap the glory and spoils of victory without the need to fight, and war came to the Mediterranean in June 1940.

But the apparent lull was deceptive as the British used the time to strengthen their forces in the region and immediately took steps to show emphatically that not only was Britain not defeated but also she and the Commonwealth were determined to take the fight to the Axis. Unable to confront Germany directly on land, the Mediterranean was the only theater in which British armies could engage any of the Axis forces. Moreover, they had the advantage of fighting the weaker of the Axis Allies, whose forces were equipped with obsolescent equipment, and against the soft underbelly of Europe there were more strategic opportunities to take the war to continental Europe.

Although the Mediterranean campaign began much as a colonial war, its strategic dimensions rapidly expanded. Germany became embroiled to protect the southern flank of the invasion of Russia and to support its ailing ally. But while an African adventure was not foremost in Hitler's strategic aims, the Axis commanders in the Mediterranean recognized that if they were successful in Egypt, ultimately Germany could win the war.

The Mediterranean theater stretched from the Atlantic coast of Africa to Persia, today known as Iran, and the border with India, and from the Alps to Equatorial Africa. For the first three years, fighting predominantly took place along a stretch of land between the Mediterranean Sea and the Sahara desert in Egypt and Libya, involving the legendary *Deutsches Afrika Korps*, commanded by General Rommel, and the British Eighth Army. The hot, dry, and dusty conditions were completely unlike anything experienced in Europe, and the vast, open spaces enabled a series of highly fluid armored battles that were more akin to naval operations.

The campaign was also peculiar because logistics were especially significant, since there were no local resources and every item the troops and their vehicles required had to be shipped from a base depot: Tripoli for the Axis and the Nile delta for the British. As one side advanced its own supply line became progressively overextended and less able to maintain the army, while the enemy retreated on its own base and supply became easier. Furthermore, marshes near El Agheila in the west and the Qattara depression near El Alamein in the east formed bottlenecks that were easily defended and could not be outflanked. An advancing army became weakest, therefore, just as the retreating army became strongest, which resulted in a series of advances and retreats back and forth across the same stretch of desert that became known as "the Benghazi Handicap." The inhospitable conditions and the almost complete absence of civilians, German SS, and secret police lead to a conflict that, while savage, was still fought with honor and chivalry, rare characteristics in a war that was noted more for its brutality and inhumanity.

The war at sea centered on the small British island of Malta. Situated just 60 miles (96 km) from Sicily and amid the Axis shipping lanes to Africa, it commanded a vital strategic position. The Italian Navy and the Royal Navy avoided a major fleet encounter but fought an intensive and costly "battle of the convoys," as the Italians struggled to maintain Axis troops in Africa and the British desperately kept Malta supplied, despite the most severe air assault of the war.

When America entered the war, President Franklin D. Roosevelt resolved that US forces would be committed to the Mediterranean while preparations were made for the invasion of northern Europe. The British–US alliance was forged in the Mediterranean theater as great armadas were amassed for invasions of north Africa, Sicily, and Italy. Although troops were withdrawn for the D-Day invasion of France, a dogged war of attrition continued in Italy until the end of the war.

The number of troops who fought in the Mediterranean was minuscule compared to the eastern front, but for the Western Allies it was the principal arena for active operations. It was also a war of innovation and the application of new military capabilities, including aircraft carriers, large-scale airborne operations, and midget submarines. The Allies also developed experience in coordinating air, ground, and naval forces and in amphibious assaults that would prove invaluable later in the war in northern Europe and the Pacific.

The military conclusion to the war did not bring peace to the region, however. Partisan and irregular nationalist forces had been active during the war, and a communist uprising occurred in the political vacuum that followed the German evacuation from Greece and Yugoslavia, while independence movements in Palestine, Algeria, and Egypt fought against the British and French colonial control. The Mediterranean war completely reshaped the region and created political problems in the Balkans and the Middle East that remain unresolved even today.

# Chronology

**1922 October 30** March on Rome – Mussolini becomes Italian prime minister

**1935 October 3** Italy invades Ethiopia

**1936 October 25** Rome–Berlin Axis signed

**1939 May 22** Pact of Steel between Italy and Germany

**September 3** Britain declares war on Germany

**1940 June 10** Italy declares war on Britain and France

**July 3** Operation Catapult, Force H attack on French Fleet at Mers-el-Kebir

**September 13–16** Graziani advances to Sidi Barrani

**September 27** Tripartite Pact between Germany, Italy, and Japan

**October 28** Italy invades Greece

**November 11–12** British Swordfish torpedo bombers attack the Italian Fleet at Taranto

**December 7** Operation Compass, Western Desert Force launch a "five-day raid"

**1941 January 19** British capture Kassala in Sudan and invade Eritrea

**February 6** Battle of Beda Fomm, Western Desert Force captures Benghazi

**February 12** Rommel and *Deutsches Afrika Korps* arrive in Tripoli

**March 7** British and Commonwealth troops begin to arrive in Greece

**March 28** Naval battle of Cape Matapan

**April 2** Rommel attacks Cyrenaica

**April 3** Rashid Ali seizes power in Iraq

**April 6** Operation Marita, German invasion of Greece and Yugoslavia

**April 13** *Deutsches Afrika Korps* besieges Tobruk

**May 1** British evacuation of Greece completed

**May 5** Emperor Haile Selassie returns to Addis Ababa

**May 15** Operation Brevity, Western Desert Force attacks Sollum and Fort Capuzzo

**May 18** "Habforce" from Palestine relieves garrison at Habbaniyah

**May 19** Duke of Aosta signs Italian surrender, formal end of Abyssinian campaign

**May 20** Operation Merkur, German airborne invasion of Crete

**June 1** British enter Baghdad and reinstate the Regent, pro-British armistice signed

**June 8** Operation Explorer, British invasion of Syria

**June 15** Operation Battleaxe, Western Desert Force attempt to relieve Tobruk

**July 10** General Dentz, Vichy High Commissioner in Syria, sues for peace

**August 25** British and Russians invade Persia to secure Abadan oilfields

**November 18** Operation Crusader, Eighth Army offensive to clear Axis from Africa

**December 8** Siege of Tobruk raised

**December 13** Naval encounter off Cape Bon

**December 17** First battle of Sirte

**December 19** Italian frogmen sink battleships HMS *Queen Elizabeth* and HMS *Valiant* at Alexandria

**1942 January 21** Rommel launches counteroffensive

**March 22** Second battle of Sirte

**April 16** George Cross awarded to people of Malta

**May 26** Operation Venezia, *Panzerarmee Afrika* attacks Gazala line

**June 21** *Panzerarmee Afrika* captures Tobruk

**July 1–26** First battle of El Alamein

**August 11–13** Pedestal convoy fortifies Malta, aircraft carrier HMS *Eagle* sunk

**August 31–September 7** Battle of Alam Halfa

**October 23** Operation Lightfoot, Eighth Army launches second battle of El Alamein

**November 8–29** Operation Torch, Anglo-US invasion of northwest Africa

**1943 January 28** Eighth Army captures Tripoli

**February 14–22** Battle of Kasserine Pass

**May 13** Last Axis troops in Tunisia surrender, end of North African campaign

**July 10** Operation Husky, Allied invasion of Sicily

**July 25** Fascist Grand Council overthrows and arrests Mussolini

**August 17** Allies capture Messina, last Axis troops in Sicily surrender

**September 3** Operation Baytown, Eighth Army invasion of Italy at Calabria

**September 9** Operation Avalanche, Fifth Army amphibious landing at Salerno

**September 12** Mussolini rescued by German paratroopers from Gran Sasso

**October 1** Fifth Army captures Naples

**October 12** Fifth Army launches offensive across the river Volturno

**1944 January 3** Fifth Army launches offensive against Gustav Line, around Monte Cassino

**January 22** Operation Shingle, Fifth Army amphibious landing at Anzio

**May 18** Polish troops capture Monastery Hill at Cassino

**June 4** Fifth Army captures Rome

**August 4** Eighth Army captures Florence

**August 26** Hitler orders withdrawal from Greece

**September 8** Eighth Army breaks through Gothic Line

**September 12** Germans evacuate Rhodes and other Greek islands in eastern Mediterranean

**September 28** Agreement between Tito and Stalin allowing Red Army to enter Yugoslavia

**October 4** Operation Manna, British intervention in Greece to prevent communist coup

**October 20** Red Army captures Belgrade, Tito's partisans capture Dubrovnik

**November 4** Greece completely liberated

**November 23** Germans evacuate Macedonia

**December 4** Athens placed under martial law

**1945 March 8** Secret negotiations in Bern for early surrender of German forces in Italy

**April 6** Tito's partisans capture Sarajevo

**April 14** Fifth and Eighth Armies attack in Po valley

**April 28** Mussolini captured and hanged by partisans

**May 1** Eighth Army captures Udine, and links up with Tito's partisans near Trieste

**May 2** German forces in Italy surrender, formal end to war in the Mediterranean

**May 6** Fifth Army enters Austria from Italy

**May 9** German forces in the Greek islands surrender

**May 12** German garrison in Crete surrenders

# Italian imperialism

## The fascist rise to power

Benito Mussolini became prime minister of Italy in October 1922 as head of the *Fassci di Combattimento*, the Fascist Party, which enabled him to assume dictatorial powers three years later. His regime inherited the colonies of Libya, Eritrea, Italian Somaliland, and the Dodecanese Islands, but during his early years, Mussolini pursued a comparatively pacifist foreign policy. While still trying to secure his own domestic support, he emphasized that fascism would try to be an element of equilibrium and peace in Europe, and secure Italy's interests by respecting treaties of mutual friendship.

But Mussolini was a grandiose leader who relied on propaganda and bombastic rhetoric to amplify the regime's achievements and exaggerate his own importance. He wished to see Italy taken as a serious power on the world stage, especially in the Mediterranean, which he regarded as an Italian lake, and in Africa, where to his chagrin Britain and France had acquired a more prestigious empire than Italy. Mussolini boasted that Italy had three times given civilization to a barbarian world, and in an excess of pompous self-indulgence, he claimed that Italians were the most solid and homogeneous people in Europe, who were destined to raise the flag of imperialism throughout the Mediterranean and make Rome once again the center of western civilization.

In reality, however, Italy was only a middle-ranking power. Weaker economically than Britain or France, and with an army that had not been modernized, Mussolini required a prestigious propaganda coup to bolster his domestic support. Taking advantage of an international situation in which Italian friendship was courted on all sides, Mussolini decided to conquer Ethiopia and establish the king of Italy as emperor. On October 3, 1935, the numerically superior Italian forces under Graziani invaded Ethiopia from Italian Somaliland. Though ineptly led, they faced little real opposition, and by May 1936, Emperor Haile Selassie was forced to leave Ethiopia. The Italians immediately combined their colonies of Eritrea, Italian Somaliland, and Ethiopia into a single federation, Italian East Africa, with Graziani, and later the Duke of Aosta, as governor-general. On May 9, 1936, on the floodlit balcony of the Palazzo Venezia, Mussolini proclaimed to a large crowd the foundation of a new Roman empire.

It was Mussolini's finest moment, but the theatrical extravagance masked deeper problems. By committing to a distant empire, Mussolini increased Italy's maritime vulnerability, especially the dependence on tenuous shipping links in the Mediterranean. Furthermore, despite Mussolini's promise of vast mineral resources and agricultural wealth, the maintenance of the empire and the vast army required to suppress it consumed thousands of millions of *lire* that would have been more profitably spent developing parts of Italy and modernizing the army. Ethiopia was never under firm control, and the brutal methods of repression, including the use of poison gas, ensured that a hostile population was always ready to rebel. Nevertheless, the victory reinforced Mussolini's confidence and the new watchword in Italy became *Roma doma*, "Rome dominates." Mussolini now had the illusion that he could continue without danger along the same path and play a much bigger role in Europe.

The Italian invasion of Ethiopia had far greater implications. Failure by Britain and France to impose comprehensive sanctions discredited the League of Nations and fatally imperiled the international system of collective security. Hitler had a graphic demonstration that belligerence in the face of international opposition could pay dividends and in the process he had a potential enemy converted into an ally. Mussolini increasingly came within the Nazi orbit and, with their common themes of nationalism, militarism, and anti-bolshevism, the not-unnatural tendency for the fascist regimes to converge began in earnest. The democracies, as a consequence, realized that they were now forced to commit to a policy of rearmament and the first steps were taken along the path to world war.

## The Rome–Berlin Axis

The Spanish Civil War offered another opportunity for Mussolini to assert the authority of fascism and Italy throughout the Mediterranean. Although this horrible war further unhinged the balance of power in Europe and encouraged a rapprochement between Italy and Germany, Mussolini maintained a deliberately confusing and contradictory foreign policy. Despite his bellicose behavior, Mussolini feared full-scale war against a real enemy because he knew that Italian strength had been based on propaganda and bluff. Mussolini promised the French Italian troops to defend against German aggression, yet he also assured Hitler that Italy and Germany had a partnership dictated by destiny and announced the Rome–Berlin Axis in November 1936 – a political understanding of friendship and not yet a military alliance.

Nevertheless, Mussolini was still widely admired as an anti-bolshevist, even by Winston Churchill. To balance his growing proximity with Germany and to cover himself in the Mediterranean he made a "gentleman's agreement" with Britain in January 1937 that recognized freedom of movement for both countries in the Mediterranean. Mussolini reaffirmed the agreement in April 1938, with little practical effect, but he made the important concession to maintain the status quo in the Mediterranean and to exchange information annually concerning any major changes or proposed changes in the strength and dispositions of their respective armed forces.

Mussolini had steadfastly promised to prevent Germany's occupation of Austria, but when Hitler announced the *Anschluss* in March 1938, without notifying the Italians, Mussolini acquiesced. He had been deceived and made to look foolish, but in the process he gained the permanent gratitude of Hitler. Nevertheless, Mussolini was now convinced that war with Britain was inevitable and, since his visit to Germany in September 1937, during which he was impressed by German power and the strength of the Nazi war machine, he was certain that Germany would be the victor. Despite their mutual distrust both Mussolini and Hitler realized that in the absence of alternative friends their regimes needed a closer relationship, and Hitler's visit to Rome in May 1938 brought both countries much closer together. At the Munich conference in September 1938, Mussolini played the role of mediator and guarantor of peace in Europe, and he basked in the admiration bestowed on him by Hitler.

Mussolini planned to bring the Balkans under Italian control, and by the late 1930s, the fascists had come to regard Albania as virtually an Italian protectorate. But Hitler's surprise invasion of Czechoslovakia on March 15, 1939, alarmed Mussolini, who feared that the Germans would next move into Croatia and the Adriatic. A German advance into the Balkans would usurp control of what the fascist propaganda had long claimed to be an Italian sphere of influence. On April 7, Mussolini therefore invaded Albania, an expedition that was notable only because of its incompetence and mismanagement and because the enfeebled condition of the Italian armed forces was now clearly visible to anyone who cared to look. Even the fascist propaganda could not completely disguise the calamity, but Mussolini's unbridled self-assuredness reached rarefied heights.

The democracies, however, now regarded Mussolini as simply another fascist tyrant, in cahoots with Hitler. President Roosevelt made his first serious intervention to halt the spread of the European dictators by offering his services as a mediator and attempting to revise American neutrality laws; Britain and France guaranteed Poland, Greece, Turkey, and Romania against aggression; and Britain also marked a significant change of policy by introducing compulsory military training. As a result of this relatively minor event, the schism between the fascist and democratic powers broadened irrecoverably, and the Grand Alliance that hoped to defeat fascism began to coalesce.

On May 22, 1939, the political and economic axis between Italy and Germany was formalized in the Pact of Steel, an alliance that committed Italy to enter immediately and unconditionally into any war started by Hitler. Mussolini responded with aggressive plans for the inevitable war but attempted to clarify that it should be delayed at least until 1942, since Italian rearmament required another three years of effort. Caught by the myths of his own propaganda and bluff, Mussolini had deceived himself over the efficiency of the Italian armed forces and now

Hitler and Mussolini at their meeting in Florence in May 1939 where the Pact of Steel was agreed. (Imperial War Museum HU48859)

found himself in a predicament, committed to a war that he knew neither his people nor his army were capable of sustaining. However, the Germans and the Italians both had a deep suspicion of each other and there was very little military cooperation. Neither side had any enthusiasm for a unified command, for agreeing on basic strategic coordination, or for any significant form of consultation, either then or at any time afterward. Despite the propaganda claims of the solidarity of the Axis, Mussolini and Hitler mistrusted each other and both intended to preserve the maximum freedom of action.

At the outbreak of war in September 1939, the Italian Army was in the same condition that it had been in 1915. Mussolini was

conscious that Italy's capacity for any major engagement was negligible, but he was anxious the world should not learn that for years his boasts had been mere fallacy. Torn between desire and reality, Mussolini concluded that neutrality was the only sensible policy for Italy. After preaching war for 18 years, however, he coined the phrase "non-belligerence," a more acceptable concept. Forced to remain on the sidelines, Mussolini was in a delicate position, so instead of concentrating on rearming and making preparations for war, he continued his policy of public works to reinforce his domestic support and wagered on German success. He would then enter the war, in time to enjoy the spoils of victory but without having taken any risk.

Hitler had no real interest in the Mediterranean, and the Pact of Steel symbolized his vision that Germany's interests would be served north of the Tyrol. He planned to extend German control down the Danube to cultivate Hungary, Romania, Yugoslavia, and even Bulgaria into a satellite zone by peaceful negotiation, in preparation for the struggle to expand the German Reich in the east. Meanwhile, Hitler repeatedly reassured Mussolini that the Mediterranean was an Italian sphere in which he would not interfere and was happy to allow Mussolini the freedom to extend his empire. Hitler vaguely hoped that Mussolini would attack Malta, but he had no desire for the Italians to embark on a full-scale campaign in the Balkans, which would unsettle the region and disrupt his plans.

Hitler gave substantial assistance to General Franco during the Spanish Civil War, and in March 1939, Franco made a Treaty of Friendship with Germany. Hitler regarded Spain as a debtor and Franco as a natural ally, and he hoped to negotiate a joint German–Spanish attack on Gibraltar to secure the western gateway into the Mediterranean and to use one of the Canary islands as a submarine base, in return for which Spain would gain control of the British colony. Franco joined the Anti-Comintern Pact, but Spain was still devastated by the ruin of war and was particularly dependent on the need to import food. Franco was therefore unwilling to commit to the fascist cause and even though Hitler traveled to Hendaye, on the Spanish border, on October 23, 1940, and met with Franco personally, the Spanish leader would not sanction a joint attack. During a nine-hour meeting, he frustrated Hitler with completely unrealistic demands of territories and equipment, after which Hitler stated that he would rather have teeth pulled than meet Franco again. Hitler toyed with the idea of launching a German parachute attack on Gibraltar and Franco prevaricated over joining forces, but the Germans were never able to provide sufficient enticement and there never was any active cooperation between the two fascist leaders (although Franco contributed forces to the Russian campaign when pressed by Hitler).

## Crossroads of the British Empire

The British had regarded naval domination of the Mediterranean as decisive in the victories over Napoleon and the Kaiser. Moreover, it had become axiomatic that control of the Suez Canal and the Mediterranean shipping lanes to India, the southern dominions, and the Far East was a vital element of the British Empire.

During the nineteenth century, the European powers had not been able to annex parts of the Near East, as they had in Africa. However, the British occupied Egypt following the battle of Tel el Kebir in 1882, and after the pacification of Sudan in 1885, continually strengthened their armed forces. Although never formally part of the empire, Britain established de facto control over Egypt, Cyprus, and the small states in the Persian Gulf, which complemented the strategic colonies of Malta and Gibraltar in the Mediterranean. The merit of this policy became evident in 1914 when the passage of Australian, Indian, New Zealand, and British troops had been essential in dealing with

the Middle East campaigns against the Ottoman Empire. By 1918, the British had established a huge military complex in Egypt, and in the post-war settlement, Palestine was placed under direct British control, while Transjordan and Iraq were established under British mandate by the League of Nations. As a result, therefore, Britain dominated an area from Egypt to the Persian Gulf.

Egyptian independence in 1922, and the termination of the Iraqi mandate 10 years later, had no appreciable impact on British control since four special security treaties for the defense of Egypt, foreign interests, the Sudan, and the empire's communications guaranteed the continued presence of British forces. Furthermore, the growth of the Royal Air Force, the mechanization of the British Army, and the conversion of the Royal Navy from coal- to oil-fired ships rapidly increased British dependence on the Middle Eastern oil fields. The Anglo-Egyptian Treaty of 1936 ensured that the British retained certain rights and on the outbreak of war on September 1, 1939, Britain invoked a clause that stated that, in the event of war, King Farouk would give "all the facilities and assistance in his power, including the use of ports, aerodromes, and means of communication." In effect this meant the virtual occupation of Egypt by the British Army.

Consequently, by the beginning of the war, the Mediterranean was a hub of British naval and military endeavor. British control was centered on Gibraltar in the west, Malta in the center, and Alexandria in the east, the home of the Mediterranean Fleet. France also exerted a strong influence around the Mediterranean through the colony of Algeria and the protectorates of French Morocco and Tunisia in north and west Africa, and Syria and Lebanon on the eastern littoral that were controlled under a mandate from the League of Nations. In cooperation with the French Navy, which dominated the western basin and secured French communication with north Africa, the Mediterranean shipping lanes would thus be secure if Italy entered the war.

# Italian propaganda, German professionalism, and Allied industrialization

## Italy

At the outbreak of the war, Italy appeared to be in an unassailable position. Italian armed forces were strategically well positioned, with bases astride the Mediterranean, and were numerically far superior to the forces opposing them. But this picture of strength was deceptive since Mussolini had made no preparation for war. The Italian armed forces had no higher-command structure or strategic plans and were equipped with antiquated armament.

The Italian Army, the *Regio Esercito Italiano* (REI), consisted of 1,600,000 men and comprised 73 divisions, including three armored, 43 infantry, and 17 "self-transportable" infantry divisions. They were, however, mere "binary" divisions with two rather than three regiments, a pretentious change that Mussolini had ordered in 1938 because it enabled him to claim that Italy had almost doubled its number of divisions. In reality the change caused enormous disorganization just as war was looming and dissipated each division's strength, while doubling the number of generals.

In October 1936, Mussolini famously claimed that Italy had an army of "eight million bayonets," but by the outbreak of war there were insufficient even for the 1.3 million rifles that the REI could muster, many of which were of 1891 vintage. The artillery dated from the First World War and a modernization program was not due to begin until 1942–43. There were no tanks, apart from feeble CV3 machines based on British First World War armored cars, and, although a few M-11 and M-13 light tanks were rushed to Africa, they were next to useless and lacked proper radio communication.

In east Africa the Duke of Aosta commanded 91,000 Italian and 200,000 colonial troops, while in Libya, Marshal Rodolfo Graziani commanded another 250,000 troops in the Tenth and Fifth Armies. Although formidable in size, they lacked proper training, equipment and, above all, were not fully motorized, problems that were exacerbated by poor Italian leadership. Both the British and Germans had a respect for the fighting ability of Italian soldiers, but both shared a contempt for the ineffectual Italian officers. Following the destruction of the Tenth Army in February 1941, the Fifth Army was dissolved and Italian forces in Africa thereafter operated alongside German divisions at corps level only, including an armored corps, under the command of Gariboldi and General Ettore Bastico. In 1942, they were incorporated into the German–Italian *Panzerarmee*, which in turn became the First Italian Army, under General Giovanni Messe, during the last phase of the fighting in Africa. Following the capitulation in Tunisia, only about 15 effective divisions remained to defend Sicily and the Italian mainland, several of which opposed German occupation following the armistice in September 1943 and fought with the Allies until the end of the war.

Although the Italian Army expanded to a maximum of 3,000,000 troops, Mussolini made no attempt to mobilize Italy's economic, industrial, or agricultural capacity. War production hardly rose above peacetime levels, and the armaments industry failed to produce any modern equipment. Despite the shortages, however, Mussolini still sent a well-equipped corps of 220,000 men to the eastern front, men and materiel that would have been more effectively used in Africa.

## Italy

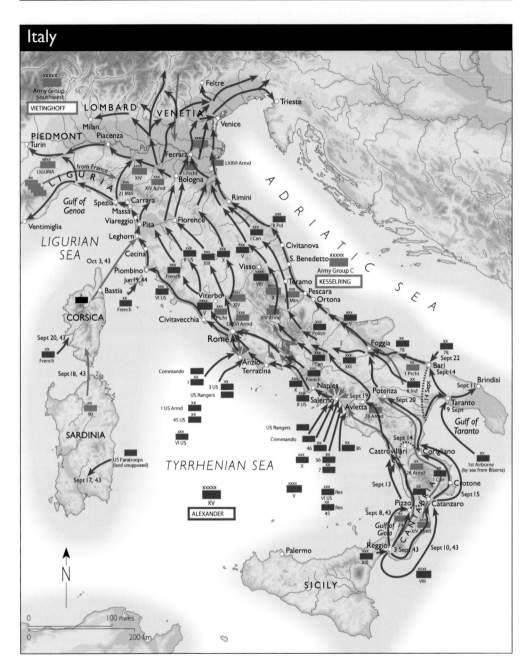

Italian fascists claimed that the Italian Air Force, the *Regia Aeronautica Italiana* (RAI), was the finest air force in the world, with 8,530 of the best aircraft. In reality the RAI comprised only 900 modern aircraft. Almost all of these were inferior in speed, performance, and armament to contemporary British planes and even included Fiat CR42 biplanes that had been operational during the Spanish Civil War. Few aircraft were equipped to operate at night or with radio communication, and their crews received paltry training compared to their opponents. More advanced Macchi 202 fighters and slow but reliable Savoia S79 and S84 torpedo bombers were flown with tenacity and great effect during the battle of the convoys, and sank or damaged many ships including the battleship HMS *Nelson* in September 1941. By mid-1943, however, the RAI numbered less than 100 modern aircraft and was hopelessly outnumbered by the superior Allied air forces.

The Italian Navy, the *Regia Marina Italiana* (RMI), under Admiral Domenico Cavagnari, was the best equipped and the most professional of the Italian armed services. The Italian Admiralty built a navy based on the policy of a "fleet in being," which assumed that the threat of powerful capital ships would be enough to deter the British from conducting an active campaign. This was in part because of Italy's inability to replace losses and because the Italian Navy could at best gain only a moral victory from a major engagement but stood to suffer a moral and materiel disaster. Postwar claims of a British "moral ascendancy" or of an Italian "paralysis of the will" were erroneous as the Italian Navy fought with determination and valor, and frustrated the Royal Navy for three long years.

Italian Cruisers on escort duty. The Italian Navy was a powerful fleet that seriously threatened the Royal Navy, but a lack of fuel oil restricted its operational capabilities. (Imperial War Museum A1985859)

Undoubtedly prestige was also a factor. The RMI possessed the largest and fastest ships with the most powerful guns, but neglected capabilities such as operational range, armored protection, seaworthiness, and accurate gunnery. The six battleships and 19 cruisers with which Italy started the war were fine ships and presented a powerful threat, but the failure to develop radar, which prevented the navy from operating at night, aircraft carriers, and an amphibious capability were serious flaws in a force that could otherwise have significantly altered the course of the war.

The RMI's smaller ships, 52 destroyers and 76 torpedo boats at the start of the war, achieved the most notable Italian naval success by maintaining supplies to the forces in Africa. The flotilla of 113 Italian submarines constituted a highly effective force, while the midget submarines or human torpedoes, a type of craft pioneered by the Italians, were the most advanced and most successful mini-submarines of all combatants during the war. The Italian "gamma men," as the frogmen were known, sank 200,000 tons of British shipping for virtually no loss. It is a compelling argument that Italy would have had considerable success if she had instead built a fleet of light and stealthy craft.

## Germany

Although an offensive in the Mediterranean was proposed as an alternative strategy to defeat Britain, Hitler and the German High Command, the *Oberkommando der Wehrmacht* (OKW), had no interest in the region and considered the campaign a sideshow to the war in Russia. However, Italian defeats in Greece and Africa threatened the existence of Mussolini's regime and prompted Hitler to send German forces to support his ally. While large forces swept through the Balkans to secure the southern flank of the Russian campaign, the assistance in Africa was limited to a rescue operation only and a special blocking force, a *Sperrverband*, was created under the command of General Erwin Rommel.

With inspiring leadership, however, Rommel welded an assortment of units without any desert experience into the legendary *Deutsches Afrika Korps* (DAK), a professional formation that was thoroughly steeped in the cooperation of all arms. Despite immense difficulties with supplies and indifference from Hitler and the OKW, with a total German force that never exceeded three divisions, Rommel repeatedly overcame superior and far more experienced British forces by using imaginative new tactics, bluff, and cunning, and deservedly earned the name of "The Desert Fox."

Rommel was nominally under the command of the Italian Commander-in-Chief, General Bastico, but he had direct recourse to Hitler and in effect personally commanded all Axis troops in Africa. The command structure was equally confusing at higher level. The Italian High Command, the *Commando Supremo*, under Marshal Ugo Cavallero, was in overall command of all Axis forces, but in December 1941, Hitler appointed Field-Marshal Albert Kesselring as Commander-in-Chief South to establish Axis superiority in the Mediterranean and ostensibly gave him control of all Axis forces. In practice the Italian and German commanders held a deep mistrust of each other and the Axis partners never truly operated as allies, with a joint command structure and a coordinated strategic plan. The potential opportunities stemming from the defeat of British power and the capture of Egypt, the Suez Canal, and even Middle Eastern oil fields were never fully appreciated. Belatedly in 1942, and without serious planning, Hitler perceived the possibility of linking the German armies advancing in the Caucasus with an advance by Rommel. By this stage, however, the tide had begun to turn as the industrial strength of the Allies began to have a material impact on the battlefield. Hitler sent 17,000 troops of the Fifth Panzer Army, under General Jürgen von Arnim, to Tunisia in response to the Allied landings in northwest Africa, but by that stage the Axis powers were in full withdrawal and the inevitable capitulation was simply delayed.

Indian troops driving Bren carriers through an Arab town. The British Army included troops of nationalities from all corners of the Commonwealth. (Topham Picturepoint M00984440)

Following Mussolini's fall from power, Hitler appointed Kesselring as Commander of Army Group C to defend Italy and sent him a further 16 divisions. Central Italy was ideal defensive territory, and Kesselring expertly and stubbornly defended every inch. Until the end of the war, the Tenth and Fourteenth Armies made a slow defensive withdrawal northward from one prepared line to another in a bloody war of attrition reminiscent of the First World War.

## Britain and the Commonwealth

General Wavell was appointed Commander-in-Chief, Middle East Command, in August 1939, but his responsibility rapidly expanded from Egypt, the Sudan, Palestine–Jordan, and Cyprus to include the whole of east Africa, Greece, Turkey, Bulgaria, Iraq, Aden, and the Persian Gulf. The High Command included Wavell's fellow air and naval commanders-in-chief, but as his was nominally the senior office, he was in practice overall commander. Wavell's responsibilities were vast. Not only was he in command of military campaigns in Egypt, East Africa, Greece, Syria, and efforts to quell the Iraqi revolt, but as the

representative of the British Government, he also had a quasi-political and diplomatic role. Although these burdens were reduced for Wavell's successors, the demands of the Middle East Command were extensive.

Initially, Wavell had command of only 50,000 British troops, concentrated in Egypt. Highly mobile, professional soldiers, they had spectacular success against the Italians, but their achievements were squandered in Greece and Crete. Reinforcements were sent to the Middle East from the UK and the southern dominions of the Commonwealth, and the Nile delta rapidly developed into a massive supply and administrative center. The Eighth Army was formed in Egypt, supplemented by the Ninth Army in Palestine and Syria and the Tenth Army in Persia and Iraq, but it was slow to adapt to the conditions of desert warfare, despite British successes in east Africa and Syria. British leadership was indifferent and failed to coordinate armor and infantry units as combined forces, errors that were repeated until General "Monty" Montgomery assumed

# Sicily

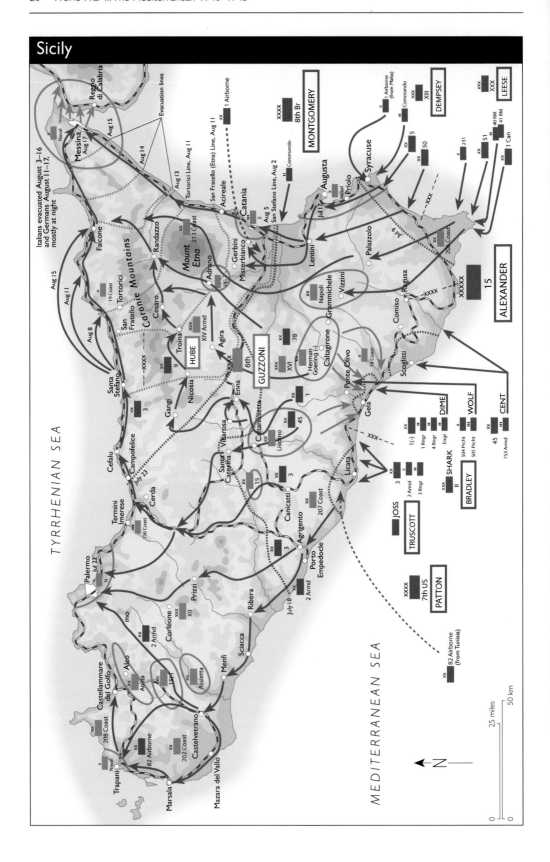

Italians evacuated August 3–16 and Germans August 11–17, mostly at night

Evacuation lines

TYRRHENIAN SEA

MEDITERRANEAN SEA

← N

25 miles

50 km

command in August 1942. With an army of 195,000 troops, 1,029 guns, and 1,051 tanks, he used the massive materiel strength to finally overcome the Axis at El Alamein, one of the turning points of the Second World War.

Following the Anglo-US invasion of northwest Africa, the Eighth Army joined with the British First Army to form the Eighteenth Army Group in Tunisia, which eliminated all Axis forces from north Africa. This force, renamed the Fifteenth Army Group, then participated in great amphibious landings in Sicily and Italy, and fought a prolonged, tenacious campaign that inched its way up the Italian peninsula.

In June 1940, the Mediterranean Fleet based at Alexandria and Force H, created at Gibraltar to replace the French Fleet, had a combined fleet of seven battleships, two aircraft carriers, 37 cruisers and destroyers, and 16 submarines. Due principally to the shortage of aircraft and submarines, the British were unable to prevent Italian convoys reaching Africa, and the maintenance of Malta both as a thorn in Rommel's side and to assist British convoys traversing the Mediterranean became a priority. But in the last three months of 1941, the Royal Navy suffered the loss of an aircraft carrier, three battleships, and Force K, the naval squadron based on Malta. With control of the sea and air, the Axis powers were able to besiege Malta with the most unremitting air assault of the war and freely ship supplies to Africa. Despite a bitter struggle, the Royal Navy was unable to regain control until the end of 1942, when it began to enforce a strangulation of Axis forces and lay the foundations for the amphibious operations.

## USA

When America entered the war, President Roosevelt effectively overruled his military advisers and determined that US forces should be committed to the Mediterranean campaign. He recognized the importance of political factors in forging the alliance with Britain and the need for US forces to gain combat experience without excessive slaughter. An invasion of northwest Africa provided the perfect opportunity, and General Dwight D. Eisenhower was appointed Commander-in-Chief Allied Expeditionary Force. Convoys of some 752 ships carried 65,000 troops from Britain and the USA in what was the largest amphibious assault of the war so far to invade Vichy-controlled Morocco and Algeria.

The invasion indicated a major Allied commitment to the Mediterranean, a theater that was dominated by the British. At their conferences in January and May 1943, Roosevelt and Churchill agreed to the invasion of Sicily and Italy, although the latter was in return for a definite British commitment to a second front in 1944. In Tunisia the fighting skills of US troops proved inadequate when they were confronted by experienced Germans, but in Sicily the Americans, in the form of General Patton's Seventh Army, came of age as a fighting force. Although the US Fifth Army fought a very determined campaign in Italy, the US Chiefs of Staff fought to restrict the numbers of US troops and succeeded even in drawing off troops to invade the French Riviera. When the Mediterranean became a unified command in December 1943, Field-Marshal Maitland Wilson was appointed supreme commander, in recognition that the majority of his troops were British.

## Vichy France

Although the French colonies in equatorial Africa sided with General de Gaulle and the Free French, the French colonies in the Mediterranean declared their allegiance to Marshal Pétain and Vichy France. After the French Armistice, the Armée d'Afrique in north Africa expanded to 250,000 troops under General Weygand, while 45,000 troops were in Syria under General Dentz. Although they were not nominally Axis troops, they were well armed and fiercely loyal to the Vichy regime, and presented significant opposition to the Allies.

# A parallel war

## Mussolini's grasp for glory

Mussolini declared war on June 10, 1940, the moment when Hitler's attack on France appeared victorious. It was also Britain's darkest hour. Although her army had scrambled back to Britain, a German invasion seemed imminent and, without France, her position in the Mediterranean looked fatally weak. So confident was Mussolini of a rapid victory that he was unwilling even to wait a few days and sacrificed a third of the Italian merchant shipping fleet, which was caught without warning in neutral ports. Unwilling and unable to participate fully in Hitler's war Mussolini planned to fight alongside Germany in what he termed a "parallel war." Ambiguously described as "with Germany, not for Germany, but for Italy," he hoped to take advantage of Nazi victories and enjoy the spoils of war to establish a dominant position in the Mediterranean.

The Italian Army launched a hapless assault into the French Alps, and Mussolini ordered an unwilling Graziani to invade Egypt from Libya. While France had been active in the war, he had good cause to protect Libya's western border with French Tunisia, but now he was able to concentrate his entire army against the Egyptian border. On September 13, Graziani cautiously attacked the scanty British force opposing him, but after advancing only 50 miles (80 km) he halted at Sidi Barrani, where he established a chain of fortified camps and settled down. Derisively the British troops termed the advance a "sitzkrieg" – a play on the German *blitzkrieg*. For Mussolini, though, military achievement was secondary to collecting his booty, as he proclaimed that he needed "a few thousand dead" to give him the right to sit at the peace table with dignity.

Despite an ignominious Italian contribution to the Axis victory over France,

Mussolini did not moderate his visions. At a meeting with Hitler at the Brenner Pass on October 4, he claimed parts of southern France, Corsica, Malta, Tunisia, Algeria, an Atlantic port in Morocco, French Somaliland, and the British positions in Egypt and Sudan. Hitler, however, had different ideas. Italian demands for territorial concessions at French expense counteracted his attempts to placate Vichy France and establish a harmonized Italian–French–Spanish alliance against Britain. Hitler encouraged Mussolini to look to Africa, which he had always seen as the natural route for Italian expansion, and in the end, Italy obtained almost nothing from the armistice and Mussolini failed to gain the glory he craved.

Moreover, Hitler was already crystallizing his plans to invade the Soviet Union. He explicitly told Mussolini that he wanted the Balkans to remain quiet so as not to arouse Soviet suspicions and that Italy was not to move against Yugoslavia or Greece. Just four days later, however, the Italians learned that German troops had entered Romania. Mussolini still considered himself the senior of the two fascist leaders, but he jealously resented Hitler's rapid victories and ascent to power. Mussolini was adamant that he had not entered the war just to be bought out at French expense or to refrain while Hitler expanded into an area that he saw as rightfully Italian. Vengeful, Mussolini reacted angrily and declared, "Hitler always gives me a *fait accompli*. This time I am going to pay him back in full." On a whim, he immediately decided to invade Greece, even though he had already ordered a large-scale demobilization.

Without any preparations and under suicidal conditions, the Italian Army crossed the border from Albania on October 28, but within a week the invasion force had been routed. The Greek Army, under General

Italian troops landing in Albania for the invasion of Greece. Their training, equipment, and leadership was so poor that they were routed by the Greek Army. (Topham Picturepoint M00983942)

Papagos, boldly counterattacked on November 14 and advanced rapidly into Albania. By January 10, 1941, the Greeks had captured Klissoura and were advancing on the port of Velona, supported by five RAF bomber squadrons. The Italians managed to stabilize the front line approximately 30 miles (48 km) inside the Albanian border, and fresh Greek attacks in January and February 1941 made little headway. Severe weather and difficult terrain conditions were crucial factors that restricted the success of both sides, but brave, determined fighting from the Greeks was matched only by almost unbelievable incompetence from the Italians, even though the senior Italian commander was replaced twice.

The Italians had shown their true mettle during fierce fighting against the Germans in 1917, but after 20 years of fascist rule, the Italian Army was dramatically more poorly equipped, trained, and led. Unsurprisingly, losses were severe, and morale was shattered. As a direct result, however, so many Italians knew what was really happening that the propaganda machine proved ineffective and the myth of Mussolini's fascism was broken.

Hitler was furious at Mussolini's petulant behavior, which had disrupted his plans for the Balkans. The region was Germany's bread basket, and the Romanian oil fields at Ploesti were the only source of oil under German control. Mussolini's venture furnished Britain with a reason for moving into the region – if British bombers menaced these strategic interests, then the entire German war effort would be threatened. Hitler, therefore, found himself forced by his truculent ally to intervene in the Balkans, to secure his own strategic interests and also to rescue Mussolini from humiliation. But the Balkans also formed a maritime base, and a German campaign there automatically drew German forces into the Mediterranean theater. Hitler's strategic focus therefore became distracted, and German forces became embroiled in fighting a larger Mediterranean campaign than he had ever envisaged. From then on, the Germans assumed the direction of affairs in the Mediterranean, and

Mussolini's idea of fighting a parallel war had to be abandoned. Thus, from the moment the Italian invasion of Albania failed, Mussolini ceased to be a war leader in any meaningful sense.

## British consolidation

When France collapsed, the Mediterranean was closed to British ships and all shipping between Britain and the Middle East, India, and the Far East was forced to sail via the Cape of Good Hope in South Africa. Ships supplying the troops in the Middle East now had to sail 13,000 miles (21,000 km) rather than 3,000 miles (4,800 km), and Bombay was now 11,000 miles (18,000 km) distant rather than 6,000 miles (9,600 km). The re-routings and associated delays increased the average round voyage from about 90 to 122 days and effectively reduced British importing capacity by 25 percent, placing an enormous strain on the merchant fleet.

Of more immediate concern to the British, however, was the fate of the French Fleet, the fourth largest in the world. The British possessed two aircraft carriers and seven battleships against the Italian's six battleships, but the Italian Navy had a significant superiority in cruisers, destroyers, submarines, and land-based aircraft. If the French Fleet actively joined with the Axis, the British would be swept from the Mediterranean. The armistice provided that the French ships would be demobilized in any port not occupied by the Germans, but it was obvious that protestations by the French commanders that the French Fleet would never be surrendered constituted but a feeble guarantee. Churchill was so concerned that he decided the powerful ships should either be placed permanently out of reach of the Germans or be destroyed. Many were located in British ports, but the majority were scattered among various African harbors, principally Admiral Marcel-Bruno Gensoul's naval squadron at Mers-el-Kebir, near Oran in northwest Algeria, which included two of the most powerful battleships afloat, the *Strasbourg* and the *Dunquerque*.

A French destroyer under attack at Mers-el-Kebir is hit in the stern by a 17-inch shell from a British warship. (Topham Picturepoint M00984452)

To enforce their determination, the British created a special force, designated Force H, based at Gibraltar under Vice-Admiral Sir James Somerville, with three battleships, an aircraft carrier, two cruisers, and 11 destroyers. Somerville arrived at Mers-el-Kebir on July 3, 1940, and gave Gensoul an ultimatum: either join the British, sail under escort to internment in a British port, sail under escort for demilitarization in the Caribbean, or scuttle his ships. Affronted by this threat, Gensoul rejected all proposals. After protracted negotiation, and under extreme pressure from the Admiralty to conclude the situation before nightfall, Somerville reluctantly opened fire. Although the *Strasbourg* and 12 other ships escaped to Toulon, the battleship *Bretagne* was sunk, the battleships *Provence* and *Dunquerque* were heavily damaged, and 1,297 Frenchmen were killed. Some 59 French warships that had sought refuge in British ports were also seized, with some fighting, and an attack was carried out against Dakar on July 7, which damaged the battleship *Richelieu*. A similar tragedy was avoided at Alexandria thanks to the good sense and cooperation of the British Admiral Sir Andrew Cunningham and the French Admiral René Godfroy. Despite the appalling news from Mers-el-Kebir, they continued to negotiate and agreed to immobilize the 11 French ships in Alexandria harbor.

The terrible calamity of Mers-el-Kebir became one of the most tragic and controversial episodes of the Second World War and caused a rift in Anglo-French relations that endured for a generation. But, for Britain, however horrifying it was to inflict casualties on those who had been allies just a few weeks earlier, if the war was to be continued, it was essential that the Royal Navy should maintain control of the Mediterranean. But, moreover, the attack also followed shortly after Churchill gave his famous "we shall fight them on the beaches" speech, and it demonstrated to the world, the Americans in particular, that though apparently on the brink of defeat, the British would fight with tenacity and courage, and would stop at nothing to achieve eventual victory.

Following the inconclusive encounter off Punta Stilo in Calabria on July 9, the only engagement during the war in which Italian battleships were involved in hostile action, the Italian Navy withdrew its capital ships to port. The British position was far more precarious. With a plethora of duties and Malta eliminated as a base, Cunningham had no choice but to be active. The Italian Navy was a serious threat that had to be neutralized, and based on the experience of Mers-el-Kebir, the British developed a plan for an aerial attack on Italy's largest and most heavily defended naval base at Taranto. In a daring and well-planned strike on the night of

HMS *Illustrious* joined Admiral Cunningham's fleet at Alexandria in August 1940 as a brand new aircraft carrier, fitted with the lastest equipment, including radar. She also had one other more basic feature that was to prove of vital importance to her, and much later to two of her sister ships, *Victorious* and *Formidable* – a 3-inch armored flight deck. (Imperial War Museum)

November 11, the aircraft carrier HMS *Illustrious* launched 21 Fairey Swordfish torpedo bombers, known as Stringbags, which although obsolete and slow, were extremely tough. Three battleships were hit, causing the *Littorio* and the *Duillo* to be laid up for several months, put the *Cavour* out of action for the rest of the war, and heavily damaged the port. The following day the undamaged ships were sent north to Naples for safety. Since they were farther from the sea lanes, they posed less danger to the British. The raid proved the futility of Cavagnari's efforts to rein in his

commanders from seeking action, and he was replaced by Admiral Arturo Riccardi. However, although the attack on Taranto reduced the threat of the Italian Fleet, it did not eliminate it and, despite the heavy losses, the Italian Navy was still a considerable force. The raid also had far wider implications. Japanese interest was intense, and a naval delegation was immediately dispatched to Taranto to study the operation and its consequences. A year later their findings were to be put to good use in the attack on Pearl Harbor.

## Conclusion

The first six months of the war in the Mediterranean were characterized by a series of relatively unconnected events. Mussolini tried, and failed, to conduct his own limited war alongside Hitler to gain the spoils of victory without any risk. He succeeded only in widening the strategic dimensions and expanded the war in the Mediterranean beyond a colonial conflict. The British, determined to stand alone against fascist aggression, strengthened their position and prepared to take the war to the Italians.

Albacore torpedo-bombers flying off HMS *Illustrious*. Although the British aircraft carrier spent only six months in the Mediterranean, she shifted the balance of naval power in the Mediterranean in favor of the Royal Navy. Her involvement in the raid on Taranto had far-reaching consequences, both locally and halfway around the world. (Topham Picturepoint M00984445)

# In all directions at once

## The first desert campaigns

Graziani's Tenth Army in Libya vastly outnumbered the 36,000 British, New Zealand, and Indian troops of Lieutenant-General Richard O'Connor's Western Desert Force (WDF) who guarded Egypt – grandiloquently described as the Army of the Nile by Churchill. But the British had years of peacetime experience of training and operating in the desert, and General Sir Archibald Wavell was not intimidated. He decided from the outset to take the offensive, using General Creagh's 7th Armoured Division – which had as its emblem a jerboa, and would soon become famous as "the desert rats" – to harass the Italians in a

Major-General Richard O'Connor, Commander Western Desert Force, and General Sir Archibald Wavell, Commander-in-Chief, Middle East, architects of the early British successes. (Topham Picturepoint 0032644)

continuous series of surprise raids. As a result, between June and September 1940, the Italians incurred 3,500 casualties and rarely ventured from the confines of their camps, whereas the British, who lost just 150 men, became masters of the desert and gained a moral ascendancy over the Italians.

This unrivaled mastery was manifest in the creation of special forces that operated deep in the desert interior. The Long Range Desert Group (LRDG) was formed in June 1940 by Captain Ralph Bagnold and was expert at driving and navigating in the desert, using specially adapted and heavily armed trucks. The volunteer force reconnoitered behind Axis lines, inserted spies, mounted lightning strikes against airfields and fuel dumps and, most importantly, maintained a close watch on Rommel's supply convoys. Russia operated closely with Popski's Private Army, a small special forces sabotage unit led by a Belgian émigré Vladimir Peniakoff, and the Special Air Service (SAS), which was formed in October 1941 by Lieutenant-Colonel David Stirling to make stealthy parachute raids and undertake sabotage and reconnaissance operations. The LRDG and SAS proved an effective combination and all three forces had considerable success throughout the desert war and continued clandestine operations until the end of the war. The British SAS Regiment continues to be one of the premier special-forces formations in the world even today.

With remarkable daring, Churchill sent reinforcements, including three armored regiments, to the Middle East during the height of the Battle of Britain and in spite of an imminent German invasion, while extra troops also arrived from Australia and India. Graziani made no attempt to move on after he had crossed "the wire" – the extensive barbed-wire fence built by the Italians on the

Egyptian–Libyan border, which became a feature of the desert war as successive armies crossed and re-crossed it – and remained for weeks in the chain of fortified camps he had established around Sidi Barrani. Wavell therefore conceived a plan to throw the Italians off balance while he dealt with them in east Africa. Because of a shortage of transport, in particular, he envisaged not a sustained offensive but a swift, large-scale raid lasting no more than four or five days. As a result, however, no preparations were made to follow up any success, a detrimental decision that would have serious repercussions.

Operation Compass began on December 7, 1941, with a two-day, 70-mile (112-km) march across the desert. After passing through a gap between the Italian camps, 4th Indian Division stormed Nibeiwa camp from the rear with 50 heavily armored "Matilda" Infantry tanks of 7th Royal Tank Regiment at the spearhead. The garrison was taken by complete surprise, and 4,000 Italians were captured almost without loss. Tummar East and Tummar West camps were also stormed in a day of triumph, while the camps around Sidi Barrani were overrun the next day. On the third day, 7th Armoured Division swept

A Special Air Service patrol is greeted by its commander, Colonel David Stirling, on its return from the desert. (Imperial War Museum E21338)

westward to the coast beyond Buq Buq and cut the Italian line of retreat. In three days 40,000 troops and 400 guns were captured, while the remnants of the Italian Army took refuge in Bardia, the first town inside the Italian colony, and were rapidly surrounded.

These astonishing results, however, were completely unforeseen and caused immense problems. As previously planned, 4th Indian Division was recalled from the desert for dispatch to the Sudan, but this led to the curious spectacle of British troops withdrawing eastward just as the demoralized Italians fled in the opposite direction. The Australian 6th Division was transferred from Palestine, but the shortage of trucks and the need to feed and evacuate huge numbers of prisoners led to a three-week delay before the operation could be resumed. Although the ingenious development of field supply dumps in the desert had alleviated, the problems of transporting supplies across long distances, the operation's success was only possible because large numbers of Italian trucks had been captured and their previous owners agreed to drive them for the British.

General "Electric Whiskers" Bergonzoli had signaled to Mussolini that, "We are in Bardia and here we stay," but three days after the assault began, on January 3, 1941, the garrison of 45,000 surrendered, with 462 guns and 129 tanks. The Matilda tanks, which were almost impenetrable to the Italian guns, were again the key to the rapid success and the Australian commander, Major-General I. G. Mackay, claimed that each tank was worth an entire infantry battalion. Even before the fighting concluded, 7th Armoured Division drove west to encircle and isolate Tobruk, which was attacked on January 21. Although just 16 of the precious Matildas were still running, they once again made the vital penetration, and the coastal fortress fell the next day, yielding 30,000 prisoners, 236 guns, and 87 tanks.

The capture of Tobruk was important because its large port allowed supplies to be delivered by sea direct from Alexandria, so O'Connor intended to await reinforcements and allow 13 Corps, as WDF was now known, to recuperate. On February 3, however, his intelligence showed that the Italians were preparing to abandon Cyrenaica and Benghazi and to withdraw beyond the El Algheila bottleneck. O'Connor immediately planned a daring initiative to combine his depleted tanks in a single column and send them across the desert interior to cut off the Italian retreat south of Benghazi. From Mechili they covered almost 100 miles (160 km) of the roughest country in north Africa in just 33 hours and came out of the desert ahead of the fleeing Italians at Beda Fomm late on February 5. In a fitting climax, the minuscule force of no more than 3,000 men and 39 Cruiser tanks held off Italian attempts to break out until the morning of February 7 when, completely demoralized, 20,000 Italians surrendered, with 216 guns and 120 tanks. Using a hunting metaphor, O'Connor signaled news of the victory to Wavell in a now famous message: "Fox killed in the open," which he sent in plain English to infuriate Mussolini even further.

In 10 weeks the Commonwealth force of two divisions advanced more than 700 miles (1,126 km) and captured 130,000 prisoners, more than 380 tanks, 845 guns, and well over 3,000 vehicles at the relatively slight cost of 500 killed, 1,373 wounded, and 55 missing. O'Connor had far exceeded all expectations, but he was confident that the way was clear for him to continue his advance to Tripoli and completely clear the Italian colony. Historians have since argued that a golden opportunity to finish the war in Africa was wasted, but recent research has shown that without an operational port at Benghazi to maintain an advance, the supply difficulties would have been immense. Nevertheless, Churchill had already directed Wavell to halt the campaign at Benghazi in favor of events that were developing in Greece, and leave only a minimum force to hold Cyrenaica.

Hitler was not aware of these plans but recognized that an Italian collapse would be fatal for Mussolini's fascist regime. He was determined to save his friend and ally, and on the very day Graziani's army was finally being destroyed, he summoned Rommel, whom he chose for his ability to inspire his soldiers, to take command of the small mechanized force on its way to Africa, the DAK. Meanwhile, *X Fliegerkorps* had been transferred to Sicily and southern Italy, from where, on January 10, it launched its first attacks, with orders to neutralize the airbase on Malta, protect the Axis convoys to Tripoli, and delay the British units advancing in Cyrenaica. Rommel flew to Tripoli on February 12 with the express orders only to defend against an expected British attack, but when the first of his units arrived two days later he immediately rushed them to the front and started pushing forward.

## The conquest of Italian east Africa

In east Africa Italian forces under the command of the Duke of Aosta had captured outposts in Sudan and Kenya and occupied British Somaliland soon after Italy had entered the war. Although they vastly outnumbered the British forces, most of whom had been raised locally, Aosta was demoralized by the Italian defeats in the Western Desert, and at the moment of Britain's greatest weakness, he unwisely adopted a defensive posture. The British had also broken the Italian Army and Air Force codes and, armed with copies of Italian orders as soon as they were issued, Major-General William Platt launched an offensive into Eritrea on January 19, 1941, with 4th and 5th Indian Divisions. After weeks of hard fighting, they captured Keren on March 27, which proved to be the decisive campaign of the battle, and entered Massawa on April 8. Meanwhile, on February 11, Lieutenant-General Alan Cunningham launched an offensive into Italian Somaliland from Kenya using British east African and South African troops with startling success. After capturing

Haile Selassie, Emperor of Abyssinia, was exiled by Mussolini in 1936 after the Italian occupation of his country. In May 1941 he was escorted back to his capital, Addis Ababa, and to his throne by Colonel Orde Wingate following a daring guerrilla campaign. His was the first country to be liberated from Axis control, but he failed to ensure its independence and was deposed in 1974. (Imperial War Museum BM1986)

Mogadishu, the capital of Italian Somaliland, on February 23, he struck north toward Harar in Abyssinia, which he captured on March 26. A small force from Aden reoccupied British Somaliland without opposition on March 16, to shorten the supply line, and joined with Cunningham's force to capture Addis Ababa on April 6. In just eight weeks, Cunningham's troops had advanced over 1,700 miles (2,735 km) and defeated the majority of Aosta's troops for the loss of 501 casualties.

Even more spectacular were the achievements of Lieutenant-Colonel Orde Wingate, later to win fame as commander of the Chindits in Burma, who commanded a group of 1,600 local troops, known as the Patriots, whom he christened "Gideon force." Through a combination of brilliant guerrilla tactics, great daring, and sheer bluff, he defeated the Italian Army at Debra Markos and returned the Emperor Haile Selassie to his capital, Addis Ababa, on May 5. British troops pressed Aosta's forces into a diminishing mountainous retreat until he finally surrendered on May 16, ending Italian resistance apart from two isolated pockets that were rounded up in November 1941.

The campaign in east Africa was important because the conquest of Ethiopia, Mussolini's proudest achievement, had been undone and for the first time a country occupied by the Axis had been liberated. Another 230,000 Italian troops were captured, and vital British forces were released for operations in the Western Desert. It was also the first campaign in which Ultra (see page 67), and the code breakers at Bletchley Park played a decisive role, providing an invaluable lesson on the impact that intelligence could have on the outcome of an operation. Success in east Africa also had an important strategic consequence since President Roosevelt was able to declare on April 11 that the Red Sea and the Gulf of Aden were no longer war zones, and US ships were thus able to deliver supplies direct to Suez, relieving the burden on British shipping.

# Greece

The victories in Cyrenaica and in east Africa demonstrated the superiority of British arms in the one strategic region where they still had the freedom of action to humiliate the fascists. The Mediterranean Fleet reinforced this notion by freely bombarding the port of Genoa on February 9, 1941, and gaining a victory over the Italian Fleet at the Battle of Cape Matapan on March 28, in which the battleship *Vittorio Veneto* was torpedoed and three cruisers and two destroyers were sunk. Wavell's successes were astonishing and were an invaluable boost to British morale during the blitz, but the radiance of victory was soon dimmed.

Churchill's attention had become focused on one of his cherished ambitions of the First World War, the creation of a Balkan front. Impressed with the resilience shown by the Greeks against the Italian invaders and under the pretext of the political and moral obligation to fulfill the guarantee given to Greece against German intervention, a cause that Churchill also knew would impress the Americans, he envisioned an alliance of Greece, Turkey, Yugoslavia, and possibly Bulgaria standing up to the German forces.

Britain began negotiating in February 1941 on the nature of assistance, but the Greek dictator, Ioannis Metaxas, was unwilling to accept British troops for fear of provoking a full-scale German invasion. His pragmatic approach might have saved the British from a futile gesture that had little chance of success and which helped the Greeks little but cost the British much. Following his death on January 29, however, the less formidable General Alexandros Papagos, the Commander-in-Chief, was persuaded by Churchill to accept British troops. Encouraged by excessively optimistic reports from Wavell and the British Foreign Secretary, Anthony Eden, Churchill thus ordered that British troops should be diverted from the campaign in the Western Desert.

After Hungary and Romania joined the Tripartite Pact in November 1940, German troops prepared to invade Greece, not so much to help the Italians but to protect the southern flank of the invasion of Russia. But, with the expansion of the Italian commitment in Greece and the growing likelihood of British involvement, Hitler decided that it would be necessary to occupy the whole of Greece. He was greatly affected by his experience in the First World War and vividly recalled the effect that the Allied front in Salonika had had on the Germans on the western front in 1918. A British front in Greece would directly threaten the rear of the German offensive in Russia and, moreover, would attack by Romanian oil fields in Ploesti to attack by British bombers. These were risks that he was not willing to accept.

Bulgaria ultimately joined the Tripartite Pact on March 1, and German troops immediately began crossing the Danube. In Yugoslavia the Regent, Prince Paul, had hesitated about joining the Pact but eventually succumbed on March 25. Two days later, however, his government was overthrown in a coup d'etat led by General Simovic. Hitler was so incensed that he immediately decided to launch a full-scale invasion of Yugoslavia as well as Greece, and on April 6 attacked both in Operation Marita. Field-Marshal Lists's Twelfth Army began the simultaneous invasion of Greece and Southern Yugoslavia from Bulgaria with seven panzer divisions and 1,000 aircraft, and on April 8 and 10, German, Italian, and Hungarian troops attacked northern and central Yugoslavia. Belgrade fell on April 13 after a very heavy bombardment that caused grievous casualties and the government capitulated four days later. Although the Yugoslav Army amounted to a million men, it was antiquated and inefficient, and the Germans occupied the rapidly disintegrating country at a cost of only 151 killed. Like vultures, Italy, Hungary, and Romania helped themselves to pieces of what they assumed, incorrectly, to be a corpse; the Croatian Ustashi nationalists and the Slovenes proclaimed independent states, and Serbia became a German puppet. The massive population changes and widespread slaughter that were a feature of the cruelest of all the internecine wars in Europe during the

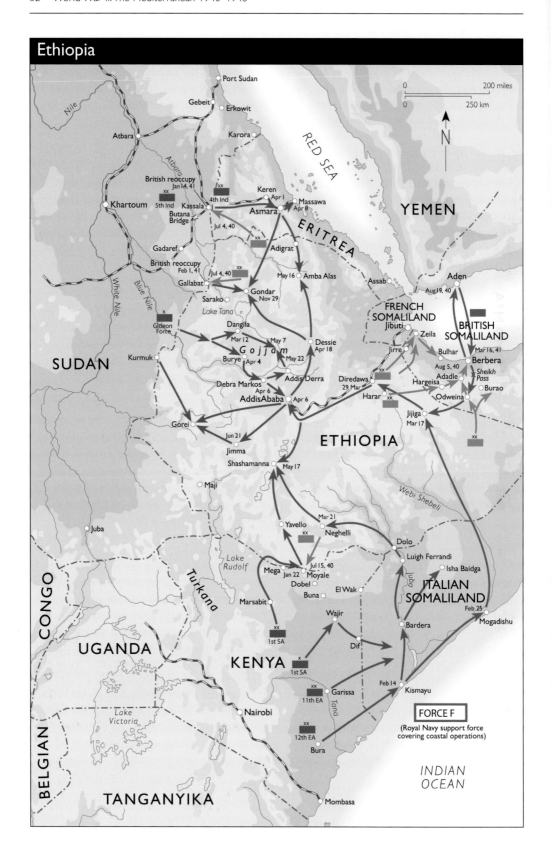

## Ethiopia

Port Sudan
Gebeit
Erkowit
Atbara
Karora
RED SEA
Khartoum
British reoccupy
Jan 14, 41
5th Ind Kassala
4th Ind
Keren
Apr 1
Massawa
Apr 8
Asmara
YEMEN
Butana
Bridge
Jul 4, 40
Gadaref
ERITREA
Adigrat
British reoccupy
Feb 1, 41
Gallabat
Jul 4, 40
Sarako
May 16 Amba Alas
Assab
Aden
Aug 19, 40
Gondar
Nov 29
Lake Tana
Dangila
FRENCH
SOMALILAND
Jibuti
Zeila
BRITISH
SOMALILAND
Gideon
Force
Mar 12
Burye
May 7
Apr 4
Gojjam
Dessie
Apr 18
May 22
Jirre
Bulhar
Aug 5, 40
Mar 16, 41
Berbera
Sheikh
Pass
SUDAN
Kurmuk
Debra Markos
Apr 6
Addis Derra
Addis Ababa  Apr 6
Diredawa
29 Mar
Harar
Adadle
Hargeisa
Odweina
Burao
Gorei
Jun 21
ETHIOPIA
Jijiga
Mar 17
Jimma
Shashamanna
May 17
Webi Shebeli
Maji
Juba
Mar 21
Yavello
Neghelli
Dolo
Luigh Ferrandi
Isha Baidga
Lake
Rudolf
Mega Jan 22 Moyale
Dobel
Buna
El Wak
Jul 15, 40
ITALIAN
SOMALILAND
Feb 25
CONGO
Marsabit
Wajir
Bardera
Mogadishu
UGANDA
1st SA
KENYA
1st SA
Dif
Feb 14
Kismayu
BELGIAN
Lake
Victoria
11th EA
Garissa
Nairobi
Tana
Juba
12th EA
Bura

FORCE F
(Royal Navy support force
covering coastal operations)

TANGANYIKA
Mombasa
INDIAN
OCEAN

Nile
Atbara
White Nile
Blue Nile
Turkana

# Greece

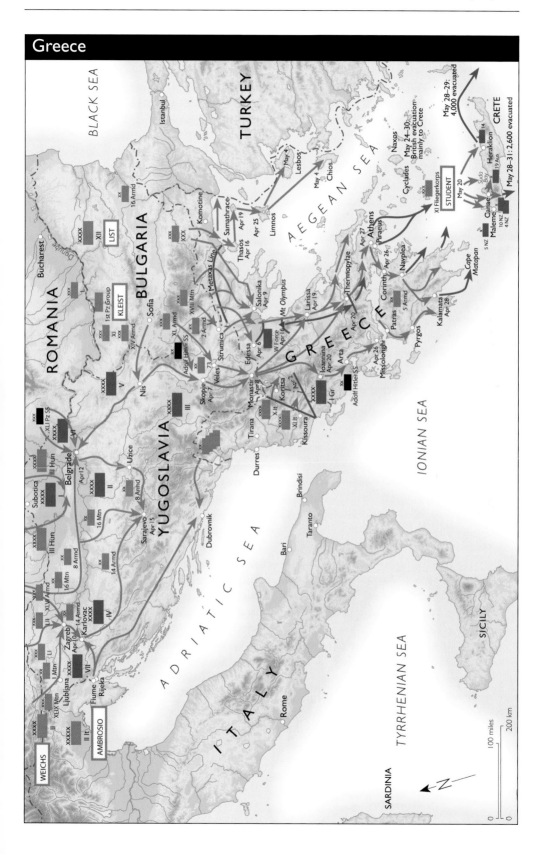

Second World War began in these first few days of fighting.

Greece was conquered only slightly less abruptly. The first British troops had disembarked on March 4 but, in a muddle symbolic of the confused negotiations, soon discovered that the Greeks had not withdrawn to defensive positions on the Aliakmon line as the British thought had been agreed. This ran from the Aliakmon river, through Veroia and Edessa to the Yugoslav border, but the two Greek armies were still in

German soldiers in Greece, April 1941. (Topham Picturepoint 0156318)

their positions on the Albanian front and in Salonika. Fifty thousand troops of the New Zealand Division, 6th and 7th Australian Divisions and a British armored brigade, supported by one squadron of aircraft, all under the command of Lieutenant-General Maitland "Jumbo" Wilson, could do little to succor the Greeks. The Germans swept south from Yugoslavia into Greece through the Monastir Gap, outflanking the Greeks in Thrace and isolating the Greeks on the Albanian front, and then pressed south into central Greece, turning the British flank. The British began to withdraw on April 10, and as the situation became increasingly hopeless, decided to evacuate on April 21. In a repeat of the Dunkirk escape, most of the troops were embarked from the beaches by April 29, but their valuable heavy equipment and vehicles were all abandoned.

Hitler decided to conclude his Balkan campaign by capturing Crete, which he feared would be used by the British as a naval and bomber base, using the one feature of his blitzkrieg army that had not yet been used – the airborne troops of General Student's *XI Fliegerkorps*. Operation Merkur (Mercury) began on May 20 with glider and parachute landings from a fleet of 500 transport aircraft. The British had failed to defend the island during a six-month occupation, and most of the 35,000 garrison, commanded by the New Zealand First World War hero Lieutenant-General Bernard Freyberg VC, had just escaped from Greece with nothing but their own light weapons. The first assault of 3,000 paratroopers failed to capture the main objective, the airfield at Maleme, but after the New Zealanders withdrew from one end during the night the Germans began the next day to land reinforcements, despite still being under intense artillery and mortar fire. Whole units were wiped out before landing, or soon after, before they could reach their weapons, and the Royal Navy balked a supplementary seaborne landing on the second night. Nevertheless, the Germans were able to land a steady stream of reinforcements, and after a week of bitter fighting, Freyberg ordered a retreat and evacuation.

The airborne invasion of Crete was one of the most spectacular and audacious events of the war, but it was also extremely costly. British and Commonwealth casualties amounted to about 16,000, on top of the 13,000 lost in Greece, most of whom became prisoners, but the loss of the equivalent of two divisions came at a time when defenses in the Middle East were already stretched thin. The Mediterranean Fleet lost three cruisers and six destroyers sunk, in addition to two destroyers sunk during the evacuation from Greece, and 17 ships damaged, including its only aircraft carrier, two battleships, and three cruisers, which proved once more that warships could not operate in waters dominated by land-based aircraft. But the Germans were badly mauled too, with several hundred planes destroyed or damaged and 7,000 casualties out of the 22,000 troops landed, more than the entire Balkan campaign. The Germans considered themselves lucky to have captured Crete, and Hitler was shocked by the losses. He concluded that the days of paratroops were over and scrapped plans for an invasion of Malta, which would have proved more beneficial to German strategy, and turned his parachute units into infantry regiments.

German paratroops, part of the German airborne invasion of Crete, parachuting onto the village of Suda on May 20, 1941. Sunken British shipping can be seen in Suda Bay, and a burning Junker Ju52 is flying across Suda Bay toward the Akrotiri Peninsula. (Australian War Memorial P0043.009)

## Rommel's first desert offensive

In Cyrenaica, Wavell had been content to use the incomplete and untrained 2nd Armoured Division and 9th Australian Division as a screening force, for he knew from Ultra that Rommel was under orders not to attack and that his forces were very weak. Nevertheless, using 5th Light Division and the Italian Ariete Division, Rommel recaptured El Agheila with ease and, seizing an opportunity, he launched an offensive on March 31, disobeying direct orders from Hitler and his immediate Italian superiors to wait for the arrival of 15th Panzer Division expected in May. Despite having no experience of desert warfare, in just two weeks, he dramatically swept across Cyrenaica until he was stopped at Sollum, reversing all of O'Connor's gains, investing Tobruk, and capturing Generals O'Connor

Rommel was never a committed Nazi and, despite his lightening advance across France in 1940, he fell out of favor with Hitler over the prosecution of the North Africa campaign. When Hitler suspected that Rommel was plotting against him, the General was offered the choice between suicide and a trial for treason. He took his own life in October 1944, and it was reported that he died of a brain seizure. (Imperial War Museum)

and Neame amidst mass British confusion. His advance gave the Germans vital airfields from which they could impose the siege of Malta, but General Halder, the German Chief-of-Staff, wrote that Rommel had gone "stark mad." Even with the reinforcements, Rommel's forces were too weak to dislodge the Australian, British, and Polish troops, "the rats of Tobruk," who were besieged in the fortress. For all his dynamism, Rommel was a prisoner of the desert and its logistical constraints. Without the port at Tobruk, his supply lines from Tripoli became dangerously attenuated, and he was unable to advance farther into Egypt.

In contrast, Churchill wanted success, and quickly. Boldly he pressed for a convoy, code-named Tiger, to sail from Britain through the dangerous Mediterranean, rather than the longer, safer route via south Africa, to Alexandria, which delivered 238 tanks that he christened his "Tiger cubs." Under intense pressure from Churchill to achieve a "decisive" victory in north Africa and "destroy" Rommel's forces, Wavell reluctantly launched two limited offensives. Operation Brevity in May, and the more powerful Battleaxe in June, using the newly arrived tanks, were hastily planned and executed. Both were costly failures, principally because of faulty British tactics. Rommel had wisely placed his screen of antitank guns and had included two batteries of 88 mm antiaircraft guns, which he used in a ground role. But, whereas the British failed to coordinate their Cruiser and heavy Matilda tanks, Rommel incorporated his antitank guns in a mobile, offensive role with his panzer regiments. In the trial of skill in armored warfare, the British incurred serious losses of 91 of the new tanks, while the Germans lost just 12 tanks. Churchill's impatience had worn thin, and despite Wavell's successes, he was replaced by General Claude Auchinleck, Commander-in-Chief India, while General Cunningham took command of the enlarged desert forces, renamed Eighth Army. But the British failed to learn valuable lessons from the experience, notably that it was antitank guns and not tanks that had inflicted the damage, and they did not evolve tactics for the next offensive.

A German 88 mm Flak Gun in action at Mersa el Brega on April 15, 1941. Although designed as an antiaircraft gun, Rommel used them as antitank guns, which were superior to any British tank and caused many British losses. (Imperial War Museum HU1205)

## Iraq and Syria

German success and growing commitment in the Balkans and the Mediterranean encouraged pro-Axis elements in Iraq to stage a coup on April 2 that brought Rashid Ali el-Gaylani to power. The Arab nationalists hoped a German victory would liberate their country, and the Arabs, from the yoke of British control and restrict the growing Jewish presence in Palestine. Encouraged by the Germans, who promised air support and to try to get materiel from Syria, Rashid Ali refused the British their treaty right to transit troops through Iraq and surrounded the airfield at Habbaniya, 25 miles (40 km) west of Baghdad. With the British fully committed in the Western Desert, Greece, and east Africa, it seemed an opportune time to move, but, in desperation, the British, fearful for their lines of communications with India and the supplies of Iraqi oil, attacked on May 2. The

10th Indian Division landed in Basra from India, and a hastily organized 5,800-strong column, Habforce, made a trans-desert march from Palestine to relieve the garrison at Habbaniya. Although German aircraft were flown via Syria to help support the Iraqis, they had moved a month too early before the Germans were able to offer effective assistance, and Baghdad was captured on May 31.

The British were alarmed by Ultra evidence that the Vichy High Commissioner in Syria, General Henri Dentz, had supplied weapons to the Iraqis and had freely cooperated with the Germans. They did not realize until later that Hitler was fixated on the impending invasion of Russia, but the fear that Germany, supported by the vehemently anti-British Admiral Darlan, who was now in control of the armed forces of Vichy France, would extend its victories beyond Crete and through Syria into the Middle East combined with the threat posed to the British base in Egypt by the Army of the Levant to convince the British to invade Syria and Lebanon. A hastily concocted force, commanded by General Wilson, launched Operation Explorer on June 8. Habforce and 10th Indian Division invaded Syria from Iraq against Palmyra and Aleppo, while 6th Division invaded from Palestine against Damascus and 7th Australian Division invaded from Haifa against Beirut. After five weeks of bitter fighting, Dentz capitulated on July 14. This tragic, regrettable episode, which cost the lives of 3,500 men, was a short but sour war that was imbued with resentment, particularly between the Vichy French and Free French Forces of General de Gaulle who fought with savage vengeance. For the British, however, the campaign consolidated their flank and guarded against any chance of German attack through Turkey.

A few weeks later, Britain occupied Iran, in unison with Russia, to guarantee the transfer of lend-lease supplies through Iran to Russia, and in the process secured its position in the Middle East. Thus, in mid-summer 1941, Germany was consolidated in the Balkans while Britain dominated the whole of the Middle East. The British commander was liberated from all other preoccupations but that of defeating Rommel in Libya, and for the first time was able to concentrate all his force on just one front. Moreover, this came at a time after Hitler launched his attack on Russia in June, when Rommel could expect no major reinforcements while Germany concentrated on the eastern front. Apart from the steadfast and spirited defense of Tobruk, including the replacement of Australian soldiers with British and Polish troops by the Royal Navy in a series of voyages during the moonless nights, a period of stalemate therefore descended on the desert war as each side reinforced its strength and prepared for the next battle.

## The Mediterranean

Malta was the only British outpost remaining in the central Mediterranean, and its presence was potentially a powerful thorn in Rommel's side. The island's strategic position, equidistant from Gibraltar and Alexandria and astride Rommel's line of communication between Italy and Africa, was pivotal. It was an invaluable aid to Vice-Admiral Philip Vian's 15th Cruiser Squadron, which escorted convoys between Alexandria and Malta, and Force H, which provided escorts between Gibraltar and Malta. However, since the arrival of the Luftwaffe in January 1941, the island had been blockaded and subjected to unremitting air raids with growing intensity, and with German forces now in Greece, Crete, and Libya, the problems of supplying Malta were even greater. Nevertheless, the men and materiel were fought through for the defense of Malta and its use as an offensive base. In June alone, the aircraft carrier HMS *Ark Royal*, once on her own, at other times accompanied by the carriers HMS *Furious* or HMS *Victorious*, flew off more than 140 aircraft for Malta. Submarines carried in urgently needed fuel and stores, but the British had been unable to strike effectively

Destroyers take men off from the sinking British aircraft carrier HMS *Ark Royal* on December 2, 1941, after she had been torpedoed by the German submarine U-81. Her loss came just a week after the battleship HMS *Barham* had been spectacularly destroyed by U-331. (Topham Picturepoint M00983945)

at the Axis convoys transferring Rommel's forces, which arrived in Africa almost without any loss, or the Italian supply convoys because of a shortage of aircraft and submarines, despite detailed knowledge from Ultra intelligence.

By the summer Malta's plight was becoming desperate, but the withdrawal of *X Fliegerkorps* for the eastern front in June eased the British position in the Mediterranean. In July Malta welcomed its first major offensive resupply convoy, Operation Substance, since January, followed by another in September, Operation Halberd. Nearly 40 merchant ships got through with only one sunk, and at a cost to the Royal Navy of one cruiser and a destroyer sunk, and a battleship, aircraft carrier, and two cruisers damaged. For a short while, the island once again became a naval base. Between June and the end of September, submarines sank 49 ships of 150,000 tons, which when added to the losses inflicted by the RAF represented a

high proportion of Axis shipping bound for Libya. The 10th Submarine Flotilla was formed at Malta in September, and the next month Force K, with two cruisers and two destroyers, was formed as a strike force to add to the offensive against Axis shipping.

By November the British had reestablished control of the central Mediterranean, and it became a time of crisis for Rommel as 68 percent of the supplies shipped from Italy failed to arrive in Africa. This situation was highlighted on November 9 when Force K completely annihilated the Axis *Duisburg* convoy of seven supply ships and two of its destroyer escorts. As a result the Italians suspended all further convoys and instead decided to use individual "fast" merchant ships and warships to transport supplies and fuel.

But Britain's strength in the Mediterranean soon came under renewed challenge. On October 27, Hitler instructed the German navy to transfer 24 U-boats from the Atlantic into the Mediterranean, the first of 62 U-boats that Germany managed to send through the Straits of Gibraltar up to May 1944. On November 14, the aircraft carrier HMS *Ark Royal* was torpedoed and sunk, followed 11 days later by the battleship HMS *Barham*, which capsized and split apart in a massive explosion,

## Mediterranean

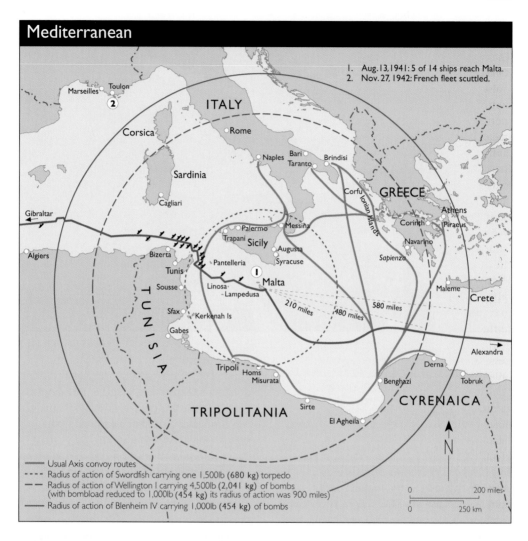

1. Aug. 13, 1941: 5 of 14 ships reach Malta.
2. Nov. 27, 1942: French fleet scuttled.

—— Usual Axis convoy routes
---- Radius of action of Swordfish carrying one 1,500lb (680 kg) torpedo
-- Radius of action of Wellington I carrying 4,500lb (2,041 kg) of bombs (with bombload reduced to 1,000lb (454 kg) its radius of action was 900 miles)
—— Radius of action of Blenheim IV carrying 1,000lb (454 kg) of bombs

with the loss of 800 men. On December 19, Force K floundered on an Italian minefield. The cruiser HMS *Neptune* and destroyer HMS *Kandahar* were sunk, but out of a force of three cruisers and four destroyers only three destroyers escaped damage. On the same morning, as Force K struggled to survive, three Italian human torpedoes of the 10th Light Flotilla were launched from a submarine. The Italian frogmen penetrated Alexandria harbor and attached charges to the hulls of the battleships HMS *Queen Elizabeth*, with Admiral Cunningham on board, and HMS *Valiant*, as well as a destroyer and a tanker. Both battleships were badly damaged and settled on the bottom, eliminating the Mediterranean Fleet's battle squadron. At the same time, other British warships were sent to the Far East to cope with Japan's entry into the war, further weakening the Mediterranean Fleet.

Hitler also appointed Field-Marshal Albert Kesselring as Commander-in-Chief, South, and ordered the transfer of *Luftflotte 2* HQ with *II Fliegerkorps* from the eastern front to Sicily, Sardinia, and southern Italy. With this powerful force, Kesselring was directed to establish a center of Axis supremacy in the Mediterranean, safeguard the routes to Libya and Cyrenaica, paralyze Malta, cooperate with the forces in north Africa, and disrupt enemy traffic through the Mediterranean. However, while Kesselring was subordinate to Mussolini, his authority was ambiguous, and confusion resulted in the Axis command structure. Italian prestige would not permit Kesselring to become supreme Axis commander, but he developed a close relationship with Marshal Count Ugo Cavallero, Chief of the Italian High Command, and a voluntary collaboration with the *Comando Supremo*, the Italian High Command. Although he commanded the

OPPOSITE The Italians pioneered the use of "human torpedoes," which were taken close to their target by specially adapted submarines. Their greatest success was on December 19, 1941, when Italian frogmen penetrated Alexandria harbor and severely damaged the battleships HMS *Valiant* and HMS *Queen Elizabeth*, which meant that the British could no longer muster a force strong enough to take on the Italian fleet. (Topham Picturepoint M00984390)

Luftwaffe, issued directives to German and Italian naval units, and cooperated with the forces in north Africa, he had no operational authority over *Panzergruppe Afrika*, as Rommel's command was now called.

## The desert campaigns 1941–42

The failure of the British summer efforts spurred Churchill's determination to gain a decisive victory over Rommel. Disregarding advice to improve the defense of the Far East, particularly the British garrison in Singapore, he rushed reinforcements to Egypt. By November the Eighth Army was significantly stronger than Rommel's forces in every category; with over 700 tanks, plus 500 in reserve and in shipment, compared to Rommel's 174 German and 146 obsolete Italian tanks, and almost 700 aircraft against 120 German and 200 Italian aircraft. Rommel had not received extra German units, and the Italian infantry divisions that had been transferred lacked any integral transport, which seriously restricted their movement. However, he had received large numbers of 50 mm antitank guns, which significantly improved his antitank capability. Rommel carefully husbanded all his supplies and planned to launch another offensive against Tobruk, but he was pre-empted by Auchinleck who launched Operation Crusader on November 18.

Auchinleck planned for 13 Corps to pin down the German outposts on the Egyptian frontier while 30 Corps, comprising the mobile armored regiments, would sweep south of these fortified positions through the desert "to seek and destroy" Rommel's armored force, which Auchinleck considered to be the backbone of Rommel's army, before linking up with the Tobruk garrison, which itself would break out from the fortress. From the outset, therefore, the two Corps would be operating independently.

A huge storm the night before the attack turned the desert into a quagmire and grounded the Luftwaffe reconnaissance flights. The element of surprise was soon wasted, however, as the British attack became disjointed and the armored brigades were involved in piecemeal battles. The majority of the fighting took place around the escarpment of Sidi Rezegh, with the Italian-built road on which Rommel's supplies were transported at the bottom and a German airfield on top, and in a repeat of the summer offensives, the British again failed to combine their armor in a concentrated blow.

Five days of hard, confused fighting, in which British and German tank formations were intermingled in the highly fluid battle, and often found themselves behind what would have been the enemy's lines, culminated on Sunday November 23 – aptly known in the German calendar as *Totensonntag* or "Sunday of the Dead," and by which name the Germans remember this battle. With skillful tactics Rommel had decimated the British, who had just 70 tanks remaining, but in a concentrated attack the next day, he lost 70 of his remaining 160 tanks. Although Rommel was victorious on the battlefield, he knew that the British were able to sustain greater losses because they had a large reserve from which to restore their strength. He therefore decided to exploit the British confusion by striking at the morale and the confidence of the British troops and their commanders, as he had successfully done previously. Rommel personally led a deep thrust with his mobile forces of the DAK to the frontier and into the rear of the Eighth Army, which he hoped would cause panic, capture British supply dumps, and relieve his garrisons on the border. Rommel's "dash for the wire" created a stampede among the British and almost succeeded as Cunningham pessimistically sought permission to withdraw, but Auchinleck was sterner and replaced him with Major-General Neil Ritchie.

Although Rommel managed to link up again with his forces surrounding Tobruk and inflicted more heavy losses on 13 Corps, which had advanced in an attempt to relieve Tobruk, his losses and the strain on his supplies became too great, and on December 7,

he began to withdraw. Rommel had to abandon his garrisons in the frontier outposts at Bardia and Sollum, but he withdrew with as much skill as he had shown on the battlefield and escaped from Cyrenaica back to El Agheila, where he had first started nine months earlier, with his army still intact.

For the first time in the war, the British had defeated the German Army. They achieved much success in the battle, finally raising the siege of Tobruk and inflicting 33,000 casualties at a cost of 18,000 British casualties. But most of the Axis losses were Italian troops or German administrative staff who surrendered in mid-January in the border posts, whereas the British casualties were predominantly highly experienced, desert veterans who could not easily be replaced. Moreover, the British had failed in their principal objective, to destroy Rommel's armored forces, and he was again recuperating on secure supply lines while the British attempted to prepare for the next offensive over extremely long lines of communication.

The resurgence of Axis control of the central Mediterranean enabled the Italians to send more supplies and reinforcements to Rommel. With more tanks and fuel, he launched an attack on January 21, 1942, and the next day his force, which now included more Italian divisions, was renamed *Panzerarmee Afrika*. His probing raid again precipitated a hasty British withdrawal, and he recaptured Benghazi, but his forces were still too weak to advance beyond the British defensive positions on the Gazala line, which ran from Gazala, 35 miles (56 km) west of Tobruk, 50 miles (80 km) southward into the desert to Bir Hacheim.

Axis domination of the air and the renewal of an intense air assault on Malta, which in March and April endured twice the tonnage of bombs that London had suffered during the blitz, enabled the Italians to resume supply convoys to Africa. Virtually free from interference, the ships could sail within 50 miles (80 km) of Malta and deliver supplies direct to Benghazi. Reinforcements, including equipment under the lend-lease program from America, were also reaching the British, and by May both sides were at a strength greater than at the beginning of the November battle. The British had 850 tanks plus 420 in reserve, including 400 of the new American Grants that had a 75mm gun and were the first tanks able to meet the powerful German Panzer IV on equal terms, while Rommel had just 560 tanks, of which only 280 were first-line German tanks. The force ratio was more balanced in the air, with 600 British against 530 Axis aircraft, although in qualitative terms, the British were inferior in nearly every aspect.

Although the British had accumulated massive supply dumps in preparation for an attack, on May 26 Rommel launched his own offensive by sweeping around the south of Bir Hacheim with a convoy of 10,000 vehicles, outflanking the British strongpoints and minefields. His bid for a quick victory failed due to the shock of huge losses inflicted by the Grants, and his army became stranded for want of fuel and ammunition. But Rommel was saved by his own resourcefulness as he personally led a supply column through the British minefields to replenish his tanks. In a bitter slogging match during the following two weeks, in an area that became known as "the Cauldron" because the fighting was so tough, Rommel again overcame the superior numbers of British tanks in a series of piecemeal battles. On June 14 Auchinleck ordered a retreat, and the British were soon in a headlong rush back to the Egyptian frontier. The British had not planned to withstand a second siege in Tobruk and had denuded its defenses, but when Rommel attacked on June 20, he captured the port and its garrison of 35,000 mostly South African troops in just one day. Besides its considerable strategic importance, Tobruk had acquired an emotional and symbolic significance and Churchill called the loss a disgrace second only to Singapore, which had fallen just three months earlier.

The watering point at Fort Capuzzo in the Western Desert. Supplies, especially water, fuel, and food, were vital in the desert, and logistics often dictated the course of battle. (Imperial War Museum)

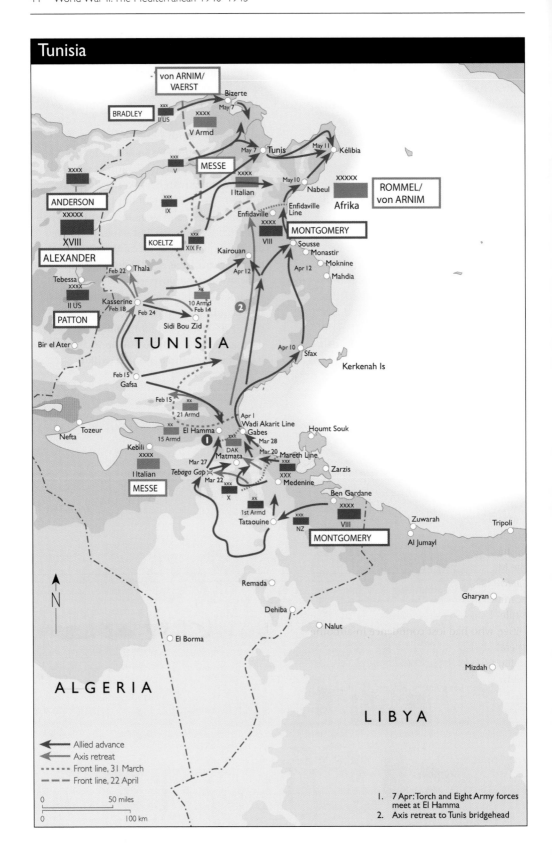

## Tunisia

von ARNIM/
VAERST

BRADLEY
xxx
II US

xxxx
V Armd

Bizerte
May 7

ANDERSON
xxxx

xxxx
V

MESSE

xxx
IX

May 7  Tunis

xxxx
I Italian

May 10  Nabeul

May 11  Kélibia

ROMMEL/
von ARNIM
xxxxx

xxxxx

XVIII

ALEXANDER

KOELTZ
xxx
XIX Fr

Enfidaville
Enfidaville
Line

Afrika

Thala
Feb 22

Tebessa
xxxx

II US

PATTON

Kasserine
Feb 18
Feb 24

xx
10 Armd
Feb 14

Sidi Bou Zid

Kairouan

Apr 12

xxxx
VIII

MONTGOMERY
xxxxx

Sousse
Monastir
Moknine
Mahdia

Apr 12

②

Bir el Ater

Feb 15
Gafsa

T U N I S I A

Feb 15

xx
21 Armd

Apr 10  Sfax

Kerkenah Is

Nefta

Tozeur

Kebili
xxxx

I Italian

MESSE

El Hamma
xx
15 Armd

Mar 27
Tebaga Gap

Mar 22

Apr I
Wadi Akarit Line
Gabes
xxx
Mar 28

xx
DAK
Matmata

Mar 20

xxx

xxx

xxx
X

Houmt Souk

Mareth Line

xxx
Medenine

Zarzis

①

xx
1st Armd
Tataouine

Ben Gardane

xxx
NZ

xxxx
VIII

MONTGOMERY

Zuwarah

Al Jumayl

Tripoli

Remada

Gharyan

Dehiba

Nalut

El Borma

Mizdah

N

A L G E R I A

L I B Y A

← Allied advance
← Axis retreat
▪▪▪▪▪ Front line, 31 March
— — Front line, 22 April

0        50 miles
0      100 km

1.  7 Apr: Torch and Eight Army forces
    meet at El Hamma
2.  Axis retreat to Tunis bridgehead

A British army truck in the Western Desert November 1, 1940, during Opration Compass, throws up a cloud of dust and illustrates the difficulties of driving in desert conditions. Navigation could be done only by using a compass and the sun, and many drivers became lost in "the blue," as the British called the desert. (Imperial War Museum E974)

Rommel captured enormous quantities of supplies and transport, and was promoted to Field-Marshal in reward for the victory, but Axis strategy struck a dilemma. It had been agreed that after Tobruk was captured Rommel would pause in favor of Operation Hercules, the invasion of Malta, but Rommel's audacious advance now offered the real possibility of capturing the whole British position in Egypt, and even taking control of the Middle East. Kesselring and the *Comando Supremo* were averse to pushing on, but Rommel was desperate to continue his pursuit while the British were still in a state of chaos. Hitler, who had lost confidence in airborne operations, and Mussolini, who flew a white stallion to Africa that he hoped to ride triumphantly into Cairo, were both in favor of the more glorious prospects. On June 24, Rommel's panzer spearheads resumed the chase, often racing ahead of retreating British units, and on June 30 reached El Alamein, just 60 miles (96 km) from Alexandria.

The crisis in British command had become so acute that Auchinleck dismissed Ritchie and took personal command of the Eighth Army himself. Panic gripped Cairo

and Alexandria, from where the Mediterranean Fleet withdrew to the Red Sea, but, in a series of limited duels during July known as the first battle of El Alamein, Auchinleck stemmed the tide of Axis advances. Rommel's forces were very weak, with his "divisions" consisting of just 50 tanks and 2,000 troops, and his soldiers were in a state of sheer exhaustion, but Auchinleck showed coolness and great skill, and came

Field-Marshal Albert Kesselring, German Commander-in-Chief South, but known to his troops as "smiling Albert" because of his cheerful disposition. He ostensibly commanded all Axis forces in the Mediterranean and Italy, and proved to be a skilled diplomat and an outstanding military commander even though he was a Luftwaffe officer and lacked command experience. (Imperial War Museum KY66846)

The tanker *Ohio* enters Grand Harbour in Malta with the destroyers HMS *Penn* on her starboard side and HMS *Ledbury* on her port side. *Ohio*'s structure had been so weakened by the repeated attacks that she was incapable of steaming on her own and needed a destroyer on either side to support her. (Imperial War Museum GM1505-1)

Sherman tanks of the Eighth Army move across the desert at speed as the Axis forces begin to retreat from El Alamein on November 5, 1942. These reliable American tanks were the first tanks used by the British that could match the armor and firepower of German tanks. (Imperial War Museum E18971)

perilously close to defeating Rommel. Nevertheless, the morale of the Eighth Army had deteriorated, and Churchill decided to appoint General Harold Alexander as Commander-in-Chief, Middle East and Lieutenant-General Bernard Montgomery as Commander of the Eighth Army. Rommel made a last and desperate attempt to reach the Nile in August, in the battle of Alam Halfa, but in his first battle, Montgomery skillfully combined the growing strength of British arms against a *Panzerarmee* that ran out of fuel, and after a few days a lull descended as both sides prepared for the next, decisive round.

Lieutenant-General Bernard Montgomery, Commander Eighth Army, wearing his famous tank beret, watches the beginning of the German retreat from El Alamein from the turret of his Grant tank on November 5, 1942. (Imperial War Museum)

The Axis blockade of Malta intensified, and on May 10, Kesselring claimed that the island had been neutralized. His declaration proved premature, but the situation became perilous despite the delivery of 61 Spitfires, which were not destroyed instantly on landing like previous arrivals. An attempt in June to run simultaneous convoys from Haifa and Suez in the east and Gibraltar in the west was a disaster, with only two of 17 ships arriving. In August another convoy of 14 ships sailed from Gibraltar, Operation Pedestal, escorted by a fleet of 44 major warships, but only five of its ships reached Malta, including the tanker *Ohio* lashed between two destroyers. The Royal Navy also incurred heavy losses in the operations, including the aircraft carrier HMS *Eagle*, with a squadron of Spitfires, three cruisers, and six destroyers all sunk. However, the convoy delivered fuel essential for Malta's defenses and to sustain the island as an offensive base at a time critical to the coming Battle of El Alamein, and food that prevented starvation and inevitable capitulation.

Rommel was also receiving a fraction of his supplies as only a quarter of the Italian shipping reached Africa. British submarines and the Desert Air Force, now consisting of 1,500 aircraft in 96 squadrons, were able to use unprecedented levels of Ultra intelligence to target the convoys and even specific ships carrying fuel. As a result fuel had to be flown to Africa, but the small quantities possible meant that Rommel's tanks were constantly in precarious danger of being halted by lack of fuel. In contrast, the expansion of British and American war production was now being felt for the first time on the battlefield, furnishing the Eighth Army with a superiority of 230,000 troops and 1,900 tanks, including 200 Grants and 300 superior Sherman tanks rushed from America, against a *Panzerarmee* of 152,000 fighting troops, comprising 90,000 Germans, and 572 tanks, very few of which could match the powerful American tanks.

Montgomery, who had a reputation for being ruthlessly efficient, inspired his men with his professional rigor and detailed tactical plans. Unlike in previous desert battles, there were no flanks that could be turned and no freedom of maneuver, which prevented Rommel from practicing the mobile tactics of which he was a master. Rather than chase Rommel back to Tripolitania, as had happened twice before, Montgomery planned to inflict a crushing defeat in a set-piece battle of attrition that would destroy Rommel's offensive power.

The battle of El Alamein began on October 23 when Montgomery launched Operation Lightfoot, so called because his infantry were attacking Rommel's massive minefields, known as the "Devil's gardens." Under the bombardment of almost a thousand guns, the largest since the First World War, four divisions of 30 Corps attacked on a front 4.5 miles (7.5 km) wide, with 13 Corps making a diversionary attack. The first week of the battle, the "dog-fight," witnessed some of the fiercest and bloodiest fighting yet experienced in the desert, but with unflinching determination, "crumbling" the enemy defenses as Montgomery called it, the British succeeded in carving two corridors through the minefields. Using skillful tactics, luck, and almost the last drop of his fuel, Rommel held up the British advance, but

Montgomery brought up reserve troops to launch Operation Supercharge on November 2, which cleared the way forward for the armor of 10 Corps to eventually break through the Axis lines.

The British night artillery barrage on October 23, 1942, which opened the Second Battle of El Alamein. Infantry carriers and ambulances waiting to move up are silhouetted against the glare from the guns. (Imperial War Museum E18465)

Although holding out for far longer than he would rightly have been expected to, Rommel could not sustain the rate of attrition, and on November 4, he decided to withdraw, ignoring an order from Hitler "to yield not one yard ... Victory or Death." Despite suffering heavy losses, including 13,500 casualties and over 500 tanks, the British inflicted a crushing defeat on the *Panzerarmee*, which no longer fully constituted a fighting force. Nevertheless, although Rommel was forced to abandon 40,000 Italian troops who had no transport, he skillfully escaped westward, successfully fending off British attempts to entrap his remaining forces. Montgomery recaptured Tobruk and Benghazi and, after a pause at El Agheila to build up his forces, finally

captured Tripoli on January 23, 1943, three months and 1,240 miles (2,000 km) after the offensive began.

## The campaign in northwest Africa

Rommel's forces were saved from complete annihilation by the Anglo-American invasion of northwest Africa, Operation Torch, on November 8, 1942, four days after Rommel had begun his withdrawal. The Allied Mediterranean strategy had been accepted in July 1942, and in a series of telegrams known as "the transatlantic essay competition," Churchill and Roosevelt finally agreed on a plan for simultaneous landings on the Atlantic coast of Morocco and the Mediterranean coast of Algeria. The Western Naval Task Force, consisting of 102 ships, sailed direct from America with 24,500 American troops under the command of Major-General George S. Patton, to capture Casablanca. The Center Task Force, comprising 18,500 American troops under Major-General Lloyd R. Fredendall tasked to capture Oran, and the Eastern Naval Task Force, comprising 18,000 British and American troops under Major-General Charles Ryder tasked to capture Algiers, sailed from Britain in convoys amounting to 650 mostly British ships.

Lieutenant-General Dwight D. Eisenhower was appointed Commander-in-Chief, Allied Expeditionary Force. His deputy, General Mark Clark, and one of the air commanders were also American, but all other commanders were British. With this mixed team, Eisenhower established Allied Forces Headquarters, the first Allied interservice HQ and a truly unified command that operated in harmonious cooperation and with a single purpose. This was fortuitous because the invasion incurred as much political and diplomatic complication as it did military complexity. Since the Vichy French forces of 120,000 troops outnumbered the invasion force, it was important to secure at least their neutrality if the invasion was to be successful. To overcome French sensibilities, since anti-British resentment was still widespread, the invasion was "Americanized" as much as possible, with Roosevelt even offering American uniforms for British troops. A confusing series of negotiations also took place, with Clark landing secretly before the

Allied chiefs at Bizerta, September 18, 1943: Air Chief Marshal Sir Arthur Tedder, Commander-in-Chief, Mediterranean Air Command; Air Marshal Sir Arthur Coningham, Air Officer Commanding Tactical Air Force, Mediterranean; General Alexander, Commander Fifteenth Army; General Eisenhower; Admiral of the Fleet Sir Andrew Cunningham, Navy Commander-in-Chief Mediterranean; General Carl Spaatz, Commander of the Northwest Africa Air Force and Major-General Walter B Smith, Eisenhower's Chief of Staff. (Imperial War Museum NA6878)

invasion to convince the French to collaborate, but excessive American caution precluded the cooperation of sympathetic local commanders.

The landings were made with complete surprise but were initially resisted, particularly at Oran and Casablanca, and especially by the French Navy, with 1,400 American and 700 French casualties. However, by sheer coincidence, Admiral Darlan, Marshal Pétain's Commander-in-Chief, had flown to Algiers the same day to visit his fatally ill son. The Americans opened direct negotiation with him, despite British reservations about dealing with such a senior Vichy and compromised pro-Axis figure, and he was persuaded to declare an armistice on November 9. This enabled British units to be dispatched to secure the ports of Bougie and Bône, to enable the overland advance to Tunisia, but the political ramifications would be far-reaching. Pétain rescinded the order, but the more immediate consequences were that Hitler occupied Vichy France and the Germans gained control of the Tunisian airfields and

were able to start transferring troops to Tunisia with the acquiescence of the French Resident-General, Admiral Estéva.

American caution at not landing east of Algiers, and the decision to reduce the number of vehicles in the invasion in favor of more troops, precluded a rapid Allied move west to Tunisia. Although the British First Army reached within 13 miles (21 km) of Tunis, by the end of November, the Germans had rushed 17,000 troops to Tunisia and in a tenacious defense stemmed the Allied forces. Hitler now recognized that a collapse of Axis power in Africa threatened not only Mussolini's regime but also Germany itself by exposing the whole of southern Europe to Allied attack. He therefore allocated massive reinforcements to the campaign in Africa on a scale far greater than ever before, at a time when men and equipment were desperately needed on the eastern front. In the next few months, the Germans committed a huge effort, including using enormous Me323 *Gigant* motorized gliders, to transfer 150,000 troops and new formidable Tiger tanks that comprised the Fifth Panzer Army, under the command of General Jürgen von Arnim.

By the end of January 1943, Arnim had pushed the Allies back and recaptured the passes in the western Dorsals while Rommel

A German Tiger tank in Tunisia. These 54-ton monsters were armed with a high velocity 88-mm gun and were far superior to any American or British tank. (Topham Picturepoint M00984402)

had withdrawn to the Mareth line, a prewar French defensive system in southern Tunisia. The strategic position was now reversed as the Germans were able to concentrate in a strong central position, and fleetingly the two panzer armies had the opportunity to strike back. On February 14, Rommel attacked the US 2nd Corps holding the southern line in Tunisia with two panzer divisions at Faid, and hoped to sweep up behind the British Army in the north. By February 20, he had broken through the Kasserine Pass and pushed on toward Thala and Tebessa, but Arnim failed to cooperate and Rommel no longer had the freedom of command to disregard the *Comando Supremo*'s instructions that he had enjoyed in the desert. The offensive was successful as a limited objective and came perilously close to driving the Allies from Tunisia, but stiffening Allied resistance and unsuitable terrain impeded the advance, obliging Rommel to withdraw for another thrust at the Eighth Army before Montgomery was able to bring forward the bulk of its strength. The Americans suffered a humiliating defeat and significant casualties, but they gained invaluable battle experience and immediately incorporated the tactical lessons.

An aerial view of Tobruk on January 22, 1941, after the Italian garrison had surrendered. Black smoke is rising from burning oil tanks beyond which, in the harbor, the Italian cruiser San Giorgio is on fire. (Australian War Memorial 106640)

Rommel was promoted to Commander-in-Chief Army Group Afrika, while his *Panzerarmee* was renamed First Italian Army, but he was one of the very few men who had been in Africa since the beginning and he was now very sick. On March 9, he flew to Germany to convince Hitler to evacuate the Tunisian bridgehead, but he never returned to his beloved DAK. Meanwhile the two British Armies had been combined into Eighteenth Army Group, under Alexander, and a unified air command formed. Although the two Axis armies formed a strong force, the Allied air and naval tourniquet prevented very few supplies reaching them. Montgomery was able to take the Mareth positions at the end of March and joined with the First Army in the first days of April. Alexander launched a final offensive on April 22, and the last German units surrendered on May 13, almost three years after Graziani had been goaded into action. Some 250,000 prisoners were captured, the largest

# Torch

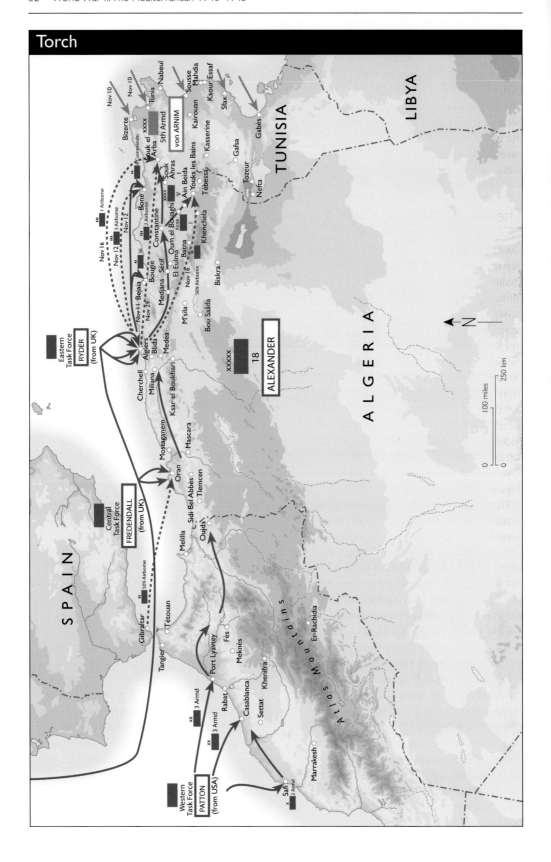

capitulation yet suffered by the Axis. Coming soon after the collapse at Stalingrad, it was a further humiliation for Hitler, but for Mussolini it was a disaster. The greater part of the Italian Army had been lost, and the Italian Empire, on which the credibility of his regime had been based, had ceased to exist. Mussolini's survival now depended entirely on Hitler.

## The invasion of Europe

The invasion of Sicily was the next logical step in the battle for the control of the Mediterranean and a possible return to continental Europe. Moreover, since free passage through the Mediterranean could not be guaranteed without its capture, Churchill and Roosevelt approved Operation Husky at the Casablanca conference in January 1943. On July 10, Alexander's newly formed Fifteenth Army Group, comprising Montgomery's Eighth Army and Patton's US Seventh Army, launched the second largest amphibious assault undertaken in Europe, landing 180,000 men, 600 tanks, and 14,000 vehicles in the first wave, supported by an enormous fleet of 2,590 ships and 4,000 aircraft.

The Italian garrison of 230,000 men consisted of weak, static coastal defense divisions and only two reconstituted German

The Captain of LCT 367, a landing craft loaded with tanks, briefs his crew before sailing for Sicily in July 1943. The use of LCTs (Landing Craft Tanks) and LSTs (Landing Ship Tanks) during the invasion enabled armor to be landed with the assaulting infantry for the first time. (Imperial War Museum NA4252)

Lieutenant-General George Patton, Commander 7th US Army, watches operations in Sicily from a town in the front line accompanied by his staff. Known as "old blood and guts" he was the US Army's most controversial and perhaps most brilliant general. (Imperial War Museum MH10946)

divisions under General Hans Hube proved formidable opponents. The landings were unopposed, but confused planning, bad weather, nervous pilots, and undisciplined naval antiaircraft fire made the first large-scale Allied airborne operation a disaster, with many troops landing in the sea. While Patton occupied the western half of Sicily, Montgomery advanced up the eastern coast, each side of Mount Etna, to cut off the Axis line of retreat across the Straits of Messina. Despite an overwhelming Allied superiority and fruitless amphibious leaps, the Germans used the rugged landscape to establish stout defensive lines to slow the British advance. Kesselring ordered a total evacuation to start on August 11, and in a brilliantly planned and executed operation, over 100,000 troops escaped unhindered with all their equipment and almost 10,000 vehicles, deflating the Allies' triumphant but hollow march into Messina a week later.

Although Allied troops, particularly the Americans, came of age fighting in European conditions, their commanders behaved with an ineptitude, jealousy, and mistrust that generated some blatant Anglo-American ill will. But the effect of the campaign on the Italian rulers was even more profound. Faced with growing unrest in Italy and the reluctance of Italian forces to oppose the Allies, the Fascist Grand Council launched a coup d'etat that overthrew Mussolini and installed a new government led by Marshal Pietro Badoglio, who had been fired during the fiasco in Greece in 1940. He immediately began secret negotiations for an armistice, but they became bogged down on the Allied resolve for unconditional surrender, a doctrine that Roosevelt had insisted on following the uneasy negotiations with the Vichy French in Algeria. A "Short Military Armistice" was eventually signed on September 3, but Hitler used the interlude to move another 16 divisions to Italy, including the crack 1st SS Panzer Division from Russia, which occupied the entire country and took control of the Italian army. Much of the Italian Fleet escaped to Malta, but the battleship *Roma* was sunk by the Luftwaffe using a new weapon, an Fx-1400 3,000 lb

(1,360 kg) armor-piercing, air-launched, radio-controlled gliding bomb. Mussolini was rescued from captivity in the mountains at Grand Sasso in a daring airborne raid led by an SS Officer, Otto Skorzeny, and installed by Hitler as head of the Italian Socialist Republic in northern Italy, but Badoglio and King Victor Emmanuelle's flight to Brindisi committed Italy to a brutal civil war, with tragic consequences.

In an attempt to exploit the collapse of Mussolini's regime, Churchill championed a campaign to capture the Dodecanese Islands. He hoped, against US wishes, to capture the airfields on Rhodes from which British bombers could attack the Romanian oil fields, to encourage the partisans in Yugoslavia and Greece, and above all to encourage Turkey to join the anti-Axis Alliance. During September, 4,000 British troops occupied eight of the islands, but the 30,000-strong Italian garrison on Rhodes was confined by the 7,000 German troops on the island. During October and November, the Germans recaptured the remaining islands and carried out severe reprisals on the Italians who had cooperated with the British. For the Allies the campaign was an unmitigated disaster since it failed to achieve any of its objectives, yet five battalions, or almost 5,000 men, large numbers of aircraft, six destroyers, and two submarines were all lost, while German casualties were negligible.

The Allies also failed to exploit the opportunity of Italian cooperation to launch a large-scale amphibious landing in northern Italy and an airborne raid to capture Rome due to American reluctance to commit to a new Italian campaign. At the Quebec conference in August, however, they accepted the principal of invading the Italian mainland almost as a continuation of the existing operations. Montgomery's Eighth Army crossed from Sicily to Calabria on September 3, followed six days later by 1st Airborne Division, which landed by sea at Taranto, and the main assault by 165,000 troops of the Anglo-US Fifth Army, under General Clark, which made an amphibious landing, optimistically named Operation Avalanche, at Salerno, 35 miles

(56 km) south of Naples. It was hoped that once ashore these forces would somehow find a way to open the road to Rome before the end of the year.

Kesselring had convinced Hitler that Italy could be easily defended thanks to its ideal terrain. The central mountainous spine, the Apennines, rose above 10,000 feet (3,000 m) with lateral spurs that ran east and west toward the coast, between which were deep valleys containing wide rivers flowing rapidly to the sea. The north–south roads were confined to 20-mile (32 km) wide strips adjacent to the Adriatic and Tyrrhenian coasts, where the bridges that carried them were dominated by the natural strongpoints. Kesselring formed the six divisions in the south of Italy into Tenth Army, under General Heinrich von Vietinghoff, but had anticipated a landing at Salerno and stationed 16th Panzer Division in the area. Despite their weakness the Germans launched a counteroffensive and after a week of fierce fighting almost succeeded in driving the Avalanche forces back into the sea. The Allies stabilized the beachhead by unleashing an overwhelming weight of firepower in the form of accurate naval gunfire and massive air

support, and by landing more reserves. Montgomery had been miffed at being given only a secondary role and was needlessly cautious in his advance – so much so that a group of dismayed war correspondents drove themselves through "enemy territory" to contact Fifth Army more than a day before Montgomery's advanced units managed to on September 16.

Two days later Kesselring ordered a fighting withdrawal to the first of the mountainous series of fortified defensive lines by which the Germans planned to defend the approaches to Rome. On October 1 Fifth Army captured Naples while Eighth Army advanced up the Adriatic coast and captured the airfields at Foggia, where the Allies established the US Fifteenth Air Force to launch strategic bombing raids against the Reich. By early October the two Allied Armies had formed a continuous 120-mile (193 km) line across the peninsula running along the

Conditions in Italy were terrible and often resembled the Western Front during the First World War. Here a mule train carrying ammunition passes a bogged-down Sherman tank in the forward positions in the Sangro area in November 1943. (Imperial War Museum NA8942)

Volturno and Biferno rivers, but in the three weeks Fifth Army alone had lost 12,000 casualties.

Henceforth, the campaign in Italy became a slow and remorseless grinding battle of attrition, and as the rain and snow turned the battlefield into a muddy quagmire the appalling struggles resembled the First World War battles. Kesselring had fortified a series of defensive lines, known collectively as the Winter Line, between Gaeta and Pescara. The western end based on the Garigliano and Rapido rivers, known as the Gustav line, was particularly strong and hinged on the great fortress Abbey at Monte Cassino. Beginning in early October, the Allies launched a series of operations to capture the approaches. However, despite some of the most bitter and desperate fighting of the war between the Western Allies and the Wehrmacht, particularly in the attempts to cross the Volturno and Sangro rivers, by mid-January 1944, the exhausted troops had still not reached the Gustav line and the last offensive petered out in a snow blizzard.

In four months the Allies had slogged their way just 70 miles (112 km) from Salerno, and were still 80 miles (129 km) from Rome. Fifth Army alone had incurred 40,000 casualties, far

On August 15, 1944, the Allies undertook the invasion of southern France, after much Anglo-US wrangling. Although troops were withdrawn from Italy, the landings were a great success and enabled supplies to be landed through the southern French ports. (Topham Picturepoint M00984374)

exceeding German losses, and a further 50,000 sick, while six experienced divisions were also withdrawn for Operation Overlord. Eisenhower and Montgomery departed to command the cross-channel invasion, and General Wilson was appointed Supreme Commander of the Mediterranean Command, in recognition of the British predominance, while General Oliver Leese became Commander of Eighth Army.

Kesselring now had 15, albeit weakened, divisions in Tenth Army vigorously holding the Gustav line. To unhinge this force, the Allies launched another amphibious landing, Operation Shingle, at Anzio, 30 miles (48 km) south of Rome, on January 22, 1944. US 6th Corps, under Major-General John Lucas, achieved complete surprise and safely landed 70,000 troops within a week, but failed to exploit the advantage. Churchill later wrote: "I had hoped that we were hurling a wild cat on to the shore, but all we got was a

Churchill described the Allied force at Anzio as a "stranded whale." After the failure of the original plan to relieve the pressure on Monte Cassino, the Allies considered a Dunkirk-style evacuation. (Imperial War Museum)

stranded whale." In contrast, Kesselring hastily improvised eight divisions into Fourteenth Army, commanded by General Eberhard von Mackensen. He resolutely counterattacked, using "Goliath" remote-controlled explosive-filled miniature tanks for the first time, and almost evicted the Anglo-US force. The beachhead was saved only by the excellent tactical use of intelligence in one of Ultra's most important triumphs. General Lucius Truscott replaced Lucas, but he could do no more than hold the defensive ring for three months.

On January 17, 5th Corps launched a simultaneous attack on the Gustav line, but it had to be called off within a month after the badly exhausted troops had advanced just 7 miles (11 km) at a cost of 17,000 casualties. The New Zealand Corps then attempted a direct assault on Monte Cassino, preceded by the questionable bombing by 145 Flying Fortresses that destroyed the famous monastery, but the 1st Parachute Division defending the heights were some of the best troops in the German army and did not even flinch. A third attack by New Zealand and Indian infantry, using even heavier air and artillery bombardments, also failed to break through, not least because the rubble created an impregnable defensive position into which the parachutists burrowed. A fourth attack, in which Alexander coordinated Fifth and Eighth Armies as an Army Group for the first time, was launched on May 11 with the aim to destroy the German armies. In an astonishing feat of arms, Polish and Free French troops seized Monte Cassino, and the Gustav line was broken in a set-piece battle. However, Clark was perhaps the most egocentric Allied commander in the war and

The liberation of Rome on June 4, 1944, was met with jubilant celebration. In front of the Coliseum, Italian civilians crowd round RAF leading Aircraftsman F Jones of Newport, Monmouthshire. (Imperial War Museum CAN2916)

instead of following orders to encircle the Germans, he was enticed by the glory of capturing Rome. Fifth Army finally linked up with 6th Corps on May 25 and made the triumphant march into Rome on June 4, but the spectacular of the first capture of an Axis capital was eclipsed by the Allied invasion of France two days later. Clark's impetuous failure enabled Kesselring to withdraw Tenth and Fourteenth Armies to the Pisa–Rimini line, 150 miles (241 km) north of Rome, the first of the next series of defensible lines across the peninsula, known as the Gothic line, which he reached in August. Alexander still had hopes to make for Vienna, but the Italian campaign had assumed a definite secondary status to the invasion of France. Six divisions were withdrawn in the summer, and when the autumn rains and mud forced operations to be suspended at the end of the year, another seven divisions were withdrawn.

The focus of operations in the Mediterranean had turned toward the invasion of southern France, Operation Anvil or Dragoon. The Americans believed that a landing on the French Riviera and an advance up the Rhône valley, complementary to Overlord, would be more effective than continuing operations in Italy. Despite vehement British objections, US Seventh Army, under Lieutenant-General Alexander Patch, eventually landed on August 15, 1944. The assault by three divisions of Truscott's US 6th Corps, followed up by seven divisions of the First French Army, was supported by 887 warships and over 2,000 aircraft. However, the three divisions and 200 aircraft of General Johannes Blaskowitz's Army Group G were too weak and too dispersed to offer any serious resistance. The Allied forces landed virtually unopposed and incurred few casualties, and with the Riviera resorts freely available for recreation, the invasion earned the derisive term "the Champagne campaign." Nevertheless, Seventh Army advanced northward rapidly and met Patton's US Third Army, advancing southward from Normandy, at Dijon on September 11.

# A modest hero

## Charles Hazlitt Upham, VC and Bar (1908–94)

Charles Hazlitt Upham is the only combat soldier, and one of only three men ever, to have twice been awarded the Victoria Cross for outstanding gallantry and leadership, the first time in Crete in May 1941 and the second in Egypt in July 1942.

Upham was born on September 21, 1908, in Christchurch, New Zealand, and was educated at Christ's College and Canterbury Agricultural College. From an early age, he was quiet, unusually determined, and developed a spirit of independence that bordered on belligerence toward authority, which he would only accept when shown that it was right. Above all Upham abhorred injustice, a characteristic that grew in intensity, and indicated the force of his personality.

Upham aspired to a simple life on the land. He spent six years as a shepherd, musterer, and farm manager, mostly on high-country sheep stations, and prior to the war was a government farm valuer. In 1938, he became engaged to Mary (Molly) Eileen McTamney, a nurse he had met at the races, but they had only a few happy months together before she left New Zealand for Singapore and London, where she remained throughout the war. While living in the harsh conditions of the rugged high country, Upham acquired the physical toughness, strong stamina, and cool temperament – as well as a large vocabulary of expletives – that would serve him so well during his war in the Mediterranean.

When the Second World War broke out in September 1939, Upham, aged 30, immediately enlisted out of a conviction that he wanted to fight for justice and stop the Nazis. His first task as a soldier, however, was more mundane. Because of his agricultural

Charles and Mary Eileen Upham in 1946, after their reunion in New Zealand. (Alexander Turnbull Library, National Library of New Zealand C22557-1/2)

training, he was ordered to lay down a lawn around Burnham Camp Headquarters in Christchurch, which he saw as futile to the war and completed under great protest because he missed bayonet training. But from the beginning of his military service, he displayed leadership, a tactical flair, and an intense desire to master the practical skills of the soldier's craft, inherent qualities that would be nourished by warfare. Promoted to corporal, Upham led his men in training exercises that he made extremely realistic and rapidly became noticed as a committed commander by both his men and his superior officers. Nevertheless, he rejected a place in an officer cadet training unit (OCTU), preferring instead to embark for Egypt with the advance party of the 2nd

New Zealand Expeditionary Force in December 1939 as a sergeant in the 20th New Zealand Battalion.

Upham was intent on learning the essentials of fighting and becoming skilled in using the bayonet, machine gun, and grenade. He showed no inclination for the parade ground, where he was well known for making a bungle of any drill, or respect for army conventions or rank. His intolerance of anything not directly of benefit to the war and his forthright, outspoken nature often led him to disagree bluntly with superior officers. Despite his insubordination and impatience to fight, in July 1940 Upham was persuaded to join an OCTU. Due to his outspoken opinions and his tendency to question almost everything, however, he was highly unpopular with the British officers. Upham was particularly critical of the lack of consideration that was given to the problems caused by tanks and aircraft, and felt that the tactics being used relied too much on the methods that had been successful in the First World War. As a result he was placed last in his course, but was commissioned as a second-lieutenant in November 1940.

Upham was posted to 15 Platoon, C Company, 20th New Zealand Battalion, tough men from the rugged west coast of the South Island of New Zealand, but he quickly won their respect as a capable officer who made them train hard but was equally concerned for their safety and comfort.

In March 1941 the New Zealand Division was sent to Greece. While the campaign

Lieutenant Charles Hazlitt Upham VC being congratulated by his platoon sergeant, Sgt. Bob May, after the presentation of the award in November 1941. (The War History Collection, Alexander Turnbull Library, National Library of New Zealand F-2108-1/2-DA)

rapidly developed into a withdrawal, Upham was seriously ill with dysentery. He was unable to eat anything but condensed milk, which his men scrounged for him from every source, and he became very weak as his weight diminished. He was soon unable to walk, but his battalion became accustomed to seeing him astride a donkey, which he insisted on using to ride along the hillsides between his section posts and headquarters.

Upham and his men were successfully evacuated to Crete, and when the German airborne invasion began on May 20, they were positioned around Maleme airfield, the center of the assault. Upham was in the thick of the fighting from the beginning and soon became celebrated among his comrades not only for his daring but also for his skill at out-thinking the enemy at close quarters. He was renowned for combining controlled courage with quick-thinking resourcefulness, and for his implacable determination to kill as many German soldiers as he could. While most medals for bravery are awarded for a single act, Upham's citation for his first Victoria Cross was for a series of remarkable exploits, showing outstanding leadership, tactical skill, and indifference to danger over nine days between May 22–30.

After four of his men were shot on May 22, Upham was possessed by "an icy fury" and personally dealt with several machine-gun posts at close quarters using his favorite attacking weapon, the hand grenade. When his platoon withdrew, Upham helped to carry a wounded man out under fire, rallied more men together to carry other wounded men out, and then went back through over 600 yards (550 m) of enemy territory to bring out another company that had become isolated and would have been completely cut off but for his action.

During the following two days, his platoon was continuously under fire. Upham was blown over by one mortar shell, painfully wounded behind his left shoulder by a piece of shrapnel from another, and was shot, receiving a bullet in the ankle, which was removed two weeks later in Egypt. Although he was also still suffering from dysentery, Upham disregarded his wounds

and remained on duty, refusing to go to hospital.

One incident, in particular, during this action typified Upham's deeds. At Galatas on May 25, his platoon was heavily engaged and came under severe mortar and machine-gun fire. They killed over 40 Germans, but when ordered to retire, Upham went forward to warn other troops that they were being cut off. Two German soldiers trapped him alone on the fringes of an olive grove, and his platoon watched a helpless distance away on the other side of the clearing as they fired on him. With any movement potentially fatal, he feigned death and with calculated coolness waited for the enemy soldiers to approach. With one arm now lame in a sling, he used the crook of a tree to support his rifle and shot the first assailant, reloaded with one hand, and shot the second who was so close as to fall against the barrel of his rifle.

During the whole of the operations, Upham showed great skill and dash, complete disregard of danger, and superb coolness even though he was wounded, battered, and very weak, still suffering from dysentery and able to eat only very little. He looked like a "walking skeleton," exhausted, and with his wounds festering, but his determination never faltered, and he had to be literally dragged on to an evacuation ship. His magnificent courage, conduct, and leadership inspired his whole platoon to fight magnificently throughout, and in fact was an inspiration to the battalion. Nevertheless, Upham was genuinely distressed to be singled out for a Victoria Cross. He believed that many others deserved the honor more than he did, and could only cope with the award and the unwelcome fame that went with it by seeing it as recognition of the bravery and service of the men of his unit. He even refused to wear his medal ribbon until directly ordered to do so. But Upham did keep a promise he made to his men in the heat of the battle and took the only five who survived death, capture, or injury to a lavish meal at Shepheards, the top hotel in Cairo.

In November 1941, Upham was promoted to lieutenant but was mortified when his commanding officer, Lieutenant-Colonel

Kippenberger, decided to leave him out of Operation Crusader because he believed that Upham was fretting for more action and would get himself killed too quickly. Experienced men like Upham were required to rebuild his battalion and after its heavy losses, he was promoted to captain and made company commander. After suffering bouts of pneumonia and jaundice, Upham went with the New Zealanders to Syria where they prepared positions to resist a possible German advance through Turkey and continued their battle training.

Following Rommel's assault at Gazala, the New Zealand Division was rushed to the Western Desert, where it joined the Eighth Army to stop his advance in the first battle of El Alamein. In these operations Upham performed five acts of conspicuous gallantry that would have earned two VCs in their own right, but three awards to one man was unheralded.

On June 27, the New Zealand Division attempted to halt the German advance at Minqar Qaim Ridge. Although the air was thick with tank, artillery, mortar, and machine-gun fire, Upham ran across the open ground from one section post to another, rousing his men to stand firm. Wearing only a soft cap, since he rarely ever wore a tin helmet because they would not fit the size of his head, to the bewilderment of his men, at one point he even climbed on top of a truck so he could identify the enemy positions that were decimating his company. The New Zealanders held off the sustained attacks but became encircled by the Germans, cutting off their line of retreat. During the night they broke out, with Upham leading from the front, inspiring his men in savage hand-to-hand fighting. His encouraging voice was heard above the noise of battle as he rushed numerous enemy vehicles, heedless of the fire pouring at him, destroying them all with grenades and regardless of wounding himself in the explosions.

During the attack on Ruweisat Ridge on July 14–15, Upham was instructed to send up an officer to report progress of the attack, but he went himself and, after several sharp encounters with enemy machine-gun posts,

succeeded in bringing back the required information. Just before dawn 20th Battalion was ordered forward, but it encountered very heavy fire from a strongly defended enemy locality. Upham, without hesitation, led his company in a determined bayonet charge. A machine-gun bullet shattered his arm, but he personally destroyed several machine-gun posts, a tank, and several guns and vehicles with grenades. Exhausted by pain and weak from loss of blood, Upham was then removed to the regimental aid post, but immediately after his wound had been dressed, he returned to his men. He held his position under heavy artillery and mortar fire until he was again severely wounded in the leg by shrapnel. Being now unable to move, Upham fell into the hands of the enemy when his position was finally overrun, his gallant company having been reduced to only six survivors, despite his upstanding gallantry and magnificent leadership.

In abhorrent conditions Italian doctors attempted to amputate his arm without anesthetic, but Upham stubbornly refused and probably saved his own life. He recuperated from his wounds in an Italian hospital and was then sent to a prisoner-of-war camp but, typifying his character and nickname, "Pug," he soon began a private war with his captors by making increasingly daring, almost desperate efforts to escape. In his first attempt, he leapt from a truck, with German SS guards firing at him. He was transferred to Germany in September 1943 and was involved in several escape plots, including an audacious solo attempt to scale the barbed-wire fences in broad daylight in which he was lucky not to be shot. The Germans eventually branded Upham as "dangerous" and in October 1944, he was incarcerated in the infamous prison fortress Colditz Castle, but even during his journey there he made another attempt that involved taking an incredible risk by leaping from the toilet window of a moving train in the middle of the night.

When Upham was liberated in April 1945, he was keen to see action again. Instead, he was sent to Britain where he was reunited with

Lieutenant Charles Hazlitt Upham, circa 1941. (Alexander Turnbull Library, National Library of New Zealand F-1993-1/4-DA)

and married Molly McTamney, who was then serving as a nurse, and on May 11, King George VI presented Upham with an official Victoria Cross. In September 1945, he returned to New Zealand to resume life as a sheep farmer.

Shortly after returning home, Upham learned that he was to receive a Bar to his Victoria Cross. The award caused much attention to be showered on him, but he modestly said only: "Naturally I feel some pride in this distinction, but hundreds of others have done more than I did. They could have given it to one of them." Upham always insisted that the military honors were the property of the men of his unit and claimed that he would have been happier not to have been awarded the Victoria Cross because it made people expect too much of him, saying: "I don't want to be treated any differently from any other bastard." He hated the popularity and remained a tough and forthright Kiwi, in spite of his fame.

A modest hero, Upham never saw himself as anything other than a New Zealander doing his duty. He was genuinely embarrassed by the publicity and accolades he received and attempted to avoid international media attention. Upham turned down a knighthood and refused to accept land offered to returning servicemen after the war. The people of Canterbury raised $16,536 by public donation to buy him a farm, but he declined the offer, requesting instead that the money be placed into an educational trust that would help the sons of servicemen attend university. Upham bought land at the mouth of the river Conway, North Canterbury, with a rehabilitation loan and, although hampered by the injuries to his arm, turned it into a successful farm through his own hard work. He and Molly had three daughters and lived on their farm for the remainder of his years, avoiding the spotlight of fame that the media occasionally tried to shine on him.

Charles Upham died on November 22, 1994 in Christchurch, New Zealand. He was a formidable soldier, and a natural leader who was able to shrewdly assess situations, weigh up risks, and quickly decide on a course of action. He was utterly fearless and tenaciously single-minded, but his implacable hatred of Nazi Germany and its allies certainly played a part in his success. When asked how he had become the only person in living memory to receive two Victoria Crosses, he just said: "I hated Germans." It was a sentiment that mellowed only slightly with the passing of years as his obituary noted: "It was said that no German-made car was ever driven onto Charlie Upham's farm."

Upham was an honorable, tough man with a strong sense of duty, who was also devoted to his wife and family. Modest and selfless, he always enjoyed the company of his old comrades, and was keenly aware of the sacrifices his generation had made to ensure that New Zealanders could live, as he put it, "in peace and plenty." Charles Upham is widely acknowledged as the outstanding soldier of World War II and without doubt remains one of the most courageous leaders of any modern conflict.

# Politics and war

## An "honorable" war

The war in the Mediterranean theater was unique in many ways, from the large-scale, ideological wars fought in mainland Europe and the Far East. The almost complete absence of civilian populations, apart from a few nomadic Arabs and Italian settlers in Africa, partisans in northern Italy or on the small island of Malta, ensured that the fighting was predominantly a purely military affair between professional armed forces, with minimal civic disruption. The relatively small sizes of the forces involved, in comparison to the overall war effort of each side, also had minimal impact on the domestic economies or civilian populations of the nations involved, except in Italy. Nevertheless, even from an early stage, the thrilling exploits of the glamorous armies, and their flamboyant, often self-adulatory commanders, were ruthlessly exploited by the Axis and Allied propaganda machines alike.

The absence of any SS, Gestapo, or secret security services also led to the notion that the war in the desert was an "honorable" war, a view encouraged by the troops themselves. Although the fighting was bitter and hard, both sides recognized their mutual struggle with the harsh conditions. Unofficial contact with the enemy, to swap supplies, pass on information about prisoners, or arrange temporary cease-fires, was not infrequent. The mutual esteem was epitomized by the song "Lili Marlene," which became a popular, and almost sacred, song with the troops of both sides. There can be few stranger sights in the war than troops of 7th Armoured Division, marching to the Allied victory parade in Tunis in May 1943, passing troops of the German 90th Light Division marching into captivity, with prisoners and victors both singing the same song with gusto. As a consequence, the war in the Mediterranean theater remains apart from the grotesque brutality, inhumanity, and widespread destruction and loss of life that forms the collective memory of World War II.

## Coalition warfare

The Mediterranean theater represents, more than other theaters during World War II, the product of coalition warfare. The British Army that fought in the various campaigns was not purely British but was, in fact, a Commonwealth force, consisting of three Australian divisions, the New Zealand division, three South African divisions, and up to eight Indian divisions, plus non-combatant troops and laborers from a host of other nationalities. However, all these troops were under the command of the British Commander-in-Chief, Middle East, and were subject to British strategic decisions, although the Australian, New Zealand, and South African commanders did have the right of recourse to their respective governments.

Although America officially entered the war following the Japanese attack on Pearl Harbor on December 7, 1941, and Hitler's declaration of war on America four days later, the relationship between London and Washington had been growing progressively closer since the summer of 1940 when Roosevelt accepted a Europe-first policy in case of war with Germany and Japan. Churchill and Roosevelt adopted this policy at their first Washington Conference, which started on December 22, and established the Combined Chiefs-of-Staff. This committee consisted of the American and British Chiefs-of-Staff, their representatives, and a number of subcommittees and joint boards, and became the mechanism through which Allied military strategy was planned and implemented.

Within a few weeks, however, fundamental differences in strategic concepts appeared that would dominate Anglo-US strategic debate. The British believed that German strength first had to be worn down before a major return to Europe through France could be mounted and the German Army decisively engaged. The best way to do this was to dissipate German forces by expanding operations in the Mediterranean and return to the continent via Italy, which Churchill referred to as "the soft underbelly of Europe." The Americans regarded operations in the Mediterranean as a diversion likely to hinder ultimate victory and were suspicious that British interests in campaigns in this theater were designed to salvage the British Empire. They believed that the overwhelming Allied resources should be used to launch a cross-channel invasion of France at the earliest possible date. Disagreements over this "second front" issue bedeviled Allied strategic planning for two years and led to friction at every level of command.

In spite of these differences, Churchill and Roosevelt formed a truly extraordinary personal and working relationship. Each held a high regard for the other and a determination to make the Alliance work, which their Chiefs-of-Staff and higher commanders shared, and genuine attempts were made to overcome the inherent difficulties of resolving priorities and making plans, in the shared knowledge that cooperation was essential for victory.

The British refused to accept a premature landing in France in 1942 but agreed to begin preparations for a landing in 1943. Roosevelt, however, required that American troops should be actively employed somewhere, anywhere, during 1942. Reluctantly, therefore, the Americans agreed to the only viable option, a landing in northwest Africa.

Allied Forces Headquarters was thus formed in August 1942 as Eisenhower's HQ for the campaign, and was the first Allied interservice HQ created equally from British and American officers. Eisenhower was an inspired choice as commander because

although he had never had an active command, or even ever heard a shot fired in anger, he had the ideal personal qualities to make the Alliance an everyday, working reality. Unlike many of his junior commanders, Eisenhower was not self-centered and had an amiable humanity that endeared him to others and fostered a harmonious, cooperative working environment among his Anglo-US staff. Few in 1943 had heard of Eisenhower or expected him to go any further, but his command worked so fluently that in December 1943, he was promoted to Supreme Allied Commander in the Mediterranean, even though it was a British-dominated theater. Eisenhower later wrote that his experience: "reaffirmed the truth that unity, coordination and cooperation are the keys to successful operations." His skill as a politician as much as a military commander was a key factor in Allied success in the Mediterranean and made him a logical choice as Allied Supreme Commander for Operation Overlord, the invasion of northwest Europe.

The Combined Chiefs-of-Staff met with Churchill and Roosevelt for a second time at Casablanca in January 1943. The Americans again pressed for a landing in France in 1943, but the British argued that by maintaining pressure on Italy, the Allies would force Hitler to divert forces from the eastern front and France to support his weaker partner. Since a cross-channel invasion was now virtually impossible, logistically, in 1943 the Americans again reluctantly acquiesced to the invasion of Sicily, but not that of Italy. When a third meeting was held in Washington in May 1943, just as operations in Africa were concluding, opinions on both sides had crystallized.

Churchill now pressed even more fervently for operations against Italy, whose collapse would strategically alter the whole war situation. But the Americans felt that they had been led down a "Primrose path," tricked into agreements in principle by the crafty British with ulterior motives, and argued that nothing should interfere with the preparations for the invasion of France, now confirmed for May 1, 1944. Seven divisions were returned to the UK, but the Italian capitulation opened, in British eyes, a plethora of opportunities. The invasion of Italy had followed the victory in Sicily as a natural succession, but operations in the Dodecanese and Balkans, assisted by the active resistance, "remorselessly and continuously in any and every area," could strike at Hitler's weakest point of vulnerability. The Americans wrongly viewed British arguments for a vague Balkan strategy as merely an excuse to avoid a major confrontation by political and military leaders who were still haunted by the losses in the First World War and who adamantly refused to countenance any changes to strategy. When operations in Italy became bogged down, the Americans even argued that the Italian campaign should be effectively halted after Rome had been captured, in favor of landings in southern France to support Overlord. Churchill's pleas for operations in the eastern Mediterranean were overruled, and although operations in Italy were allowed to continue, the British continued to argue bitterly against the French Riviera landings. They were eventually launched 10 weeks after Overlord, against minimal opposition, to ensure sufficient ports to supply the armies in France. But Churchill was bitterly disappointed that the 11 divisions withdrawn were not used to break through the Ljubljana gap into Austria.

Eisenhower's Allied Forces Headquarters was a new type of command, a truly integrated structure fundamentally different from earlier attempts at liaison or the Allied command of World War I. Despite two years of almost constant wrangling, Eisenhower commanded with frankness, earnestness, and goodwill, and gained a reputation as a first-class military organizer and skilled diplomat. As a result there developed an atmosphere of cohesion, in which British officers worked under Americans of lesser rank, and vice versa, and did so willingly for the good of the cause, which led to

friendships and procedures that contributed immensely to the smooth running of what otherwise could easily have become a troublesome procedure of managing the Anglo-US Alliance.

The inter-Allied collaboration that developed in the Mediterranean also prepared the way for the success of the Supreme Headquarters Allied Expeditionary Forces (SHAEF), which commanded the Allied armies fighting in northwest Europe in 1944–45, and for the success of the North Atlantic Treaty Organization (NATO) in the decades after the war. The "special relationship" between the UK and American governments that continues in various strengths still today also owes its roots to the relationship that developed between the Allies during the war in the Mediterranean theater.

Undoubtedly, Hitler and Mussolini had immense mutual respect and admiration. They spoke frequently, often appeared together in public to publicize their collaboration, which was bound in a series of treaties, and to the end Hitler showed complete loyalty to his fellow fascist dictator. However, this high opinion was not shared by their respective peoples or by their military commanders.

Germany and Italy had fought on opposing sides during World War I, and the antipathy between their peoples had not died. Unlike the British and Americans, who share many common traits, the Germans considered Italians to be incompetent and unreliable, while Italians thought the Germans to be overbearing barbarians, and they viewed each other with disdain. Most Italians did not share the Nazi ideology and disapproved of the ruthless treatment of the Jews, often refusing to turn over the Jews in Italian-controlled areas, so the relationship between the two allies was always strained.

The scornful attitude was most prevalent among the military leadership. Despite their proximity and the fact that German and Italian soldiers fought alongside each other in the Mediterranean and on the eastern front, there were no German–Italian joint institutions comparable to the Anglo-US Combined Chiefs-of-Staff. Tripartite military commissions were established by Germany, Italy and Japan in the winter of 1941–42, but their purpose was more for propaganda value. In practice there was extraordinarily little strategic coordination of military or diplomatic activities between any of the Axis powers during the war.

Mussolini entered the war only when he thought it was about to end, and thereafter pursued a war in isolation from his German ally. When Hitler invaded Romania, in preparation for the invasion of Russia, without informing Mussolini, the Duce in turn invaded Greece simply to pay him back. The rapid deterioration of the Italian position, however, extinguished Mussolini's ability to conduct war independently. He was forced to accept German help, but Hitler saw the Mediterranean as an Italian sphere of interest and strategically unimportant, and sent sufficient German troops in a rescue mission only to prevent an Italian collapse.

Rommel was openly contemptuous of his Italian commanders and blatantly disregarded the Italian command structure by seeking direct recourse to Hitler. Mussolini was, nevertheless, always nervous about German attempts to take control of the Italian high command. When Kesselring was appointed Commander-in-Chief, South, Italian prestige would not permit him to become supreme Axis commander. Kesselring was subordinate to the Duce and had a mixed German and Italian staff that worked in conjunction with the *Comando Supremo*, the Italian High Command, but his authority was ambiguous and contributed to the confusing Axis command structure in the Mediterranean.

Neither Hitler nor Mussolini had the slightest interest in cooperation, each preferring to direct his own national war effort entirely independently of the other. In 1940–41 there were significant opportunities for combined Axis operations in the Mediterranean, notably against Malta or the small British force in Egypt. If Hitler had been prepared to commit the full weight of the Wehrmacht against the scanty defenses,

it is highly likely that he would have been rewarded with strategic success, but the campaign had no ideological attraction. Even in 1942 when, at the height of Rommel's advances in Africa and the German Army's advance through the southern Caucasus in Russia, there appeared briefly the opportunity for the two forces to meet in the Middle East with a Japanese army advancing from Burma, Hitler was unwilling to coordinate with his allies. Only when disaster appeared imminent and Germany itself threatened was Hitler prepared to commit significant forces to the Mediterranean, by which time Italy was already lost.

## Ultra

Ultra was the code name given by the British to the new and highly secret intelligence produced by the decryption of intercepted German radio messages enciphered on the Enigma machine. The Enigma machines resembled a large and clumsy portable typewriter but were compact and sturdy, and were extremely simple to use. They were thus ideally suited for operational conditions and were used widely by all three German armed services, the SS, the Abwehr, and the German State Railways. Depressing a key worked a series of rotors and an electrical circuit that randomly allotted another letter, which would not be repeated in some 150 trillion depressions. The Germans therefore believed that their codes were completely unbreakable, a conviction that was never seriously questioned throughout the war.

Ultra had its source in the late 1920s when the German armed forces bought the rights to a civilian version of Enigma. Hans-Thilo Schmidt, an anti-Nazi member of the defense ministry, gave details of the Enigma to Captain Bertrand of the French military cryptographic bureau, who in turn shared the information with the Poles. By the late 1930s, they were reading many cipher signals but, anticipating the German invasion, in July 1939, they presented all their research and a reconstructed Enigma machine to the British. By this stage British cryptographers were aware of Enigma, and the potential military advantages of breaking its cipher, and established a group of university mathematicians at the Government Code and Cipher School (GCCS) at Bletchley Park. Initially about 120 people were working on this mission, but as their success extended, the number of staff increased to nearly 7,000 by the beginning of 1944.

The first regular decryption of Luftwaffe signals began on May 21, 1940, but beginning in the summer of 1941, this success was extended to the Enigma keys used by the German Navy, Army, and High Command. As a result the number of enemy signals decrypted rose steadily from a few hundred a week during the winter of 1940–41 to 4,000 a day by the end of 1942, and remained at that level until the end of the war. Moreover, highly secret Special Liaison Units were formed in the field, in the headquarters of commanders cleared to receive Ultra, with direct communications to Bletchley Park. The cryptographers meanwhile established the security procedures and acquired the expertise in collating and interpreting the translated decryptions that were all essential for the flow of intelligence to be put to effective operational use. Enigma was an integral component of the German command system at all levels, and most decryptions were dispatched with little delay, usually about six hours after the original German signal. The quality and value of the derived intelligence thus progressively improved as the cryptographers continuously struggled to ensure their mastery as the Germans regularly changed and improved their keys.

These innovations, of fundamental significance for the future of Ultra, were established just as Rommel arrived in Africa in February 1941. Immediately the British realized that the quantity and quality of information gathered through Ultra could provide field commanders with intelligence of immediate and critical value. The first convincing demonstration of this potential

in operational conditions came in May 1941, when the entire plan for the German airborne capture of Crete was decrypted two weeks before the invasion took place. However, although the British defenders were completely forewarned, operations in Crete showed the fundamental weakness of Ultra as tactical intelligence.

The number and quality of intercepts and the speed with which the decrypted messages were sent were greater than ever, the record being just three hours and 25 minutes after the original German signal, but in the midst of battle, they were nonetheless obsolete and of little value. Freyberg, the island's commander, had expected the main assault to come by sea and had disposed his troops accordingly. But his troops were bereft of any arms, equipment, and transport and thus lacked the flexibility to deal with the fluctuating situation revealed by Ultra. Moreover, throughout the war the British took immense pains to avoid arousing enemy suspicions, imposing strict secrecy on the Ultra production process and strict regulations against carelessness in the distribution and use of Ultra intelligence. Although Freyberg was privy to Ultra, which was sent to him personally even though his was not an Army command, he was expressly forbidden to make tactical use of it without corroborating intelligence. So invaluable was this source to the British war effort that Churchill judged it better to lose the battle of Crete than to risk the Ultra secret being compromised. In view of the invaluable contribution that Ultra made to the victory at sea in the following year, this was undoubtedly a wise decision.

By the time of the Battle of Alam Halfa in September 1942, the British had learned to appreciate Ultra's greatest potential contribution to victory: military strategy based on the logistical analysis of successive supply returns. The unspectacular accumulation of evidence about the German supply situation, which did not depend for its value on being up to the minute, proved more effective because it enabled long-term trends to be analyzed and pressure brought

Colonel William Slim commanded Indian troops in east Africa and Syria. He could speak in their native languages and held the devotion of his troops, who called him "Uncle Bill," while his physical presence, with his bulldog jaw, inspired tremendous confidence. He proved himself an exceptional commander and went on to achieve notable victories in Burma. (Imperial War Museum NA15123)

to bear at vulnerable points. The regular information provided about Rommel's petrol and ammunition supplies gave forewarning of convoys and enabled the British to target even specific ships carrying particularly valuable cargoes. Tank movements and aircraft sorties were thus restricted, while the regular equipment returns enabled a constant monitoring of German combat readiness. Rommel signaled his plan to Hitler on August 15, but two days later, Montgomery also had a copy. This enabled Montgomery to take measures to frustrate them, which gave credence to the "Montgomery legend," but the interdiction of Rommel's supplies was so complete that the DAK's tanks were immobilized.

Without Ultra the British would probably have failed to prevent Rommel from taking Cairo and Alexandria – if not at the end of 1941, when it first exerted a direct influence on the land battles in the Western Desert, then certainly after his victory in the summer of 1942, when it made a still more decisive contribution. The intimate relationship between intelligence and operations lasted until the end of the war and proved invaluable in Italy and in northwest Europe. Ultra revealed that Hitler had decided to hold the Italian peninsula, that lines of resistance had been ordered, and through a continuous and detailed record of the German order of battle, that Hitler was withdrawing troops from other fronts to reinforce Italy. The Italian campaign was thus planned with authority and in the knowledge that the political and military directive to Eisenhower to attract as many German troops to Italy and hold them there was being fulfilled.

There can hardly be any doubt that the regular provision of absolutely reliable, if sometimes incomplete, intelligence about the enemy's actions, resources, and intentions significantly contributed to eventual Allied victory. The experience of decrypting, analyzing, and making operational use of Ultra intelligence during the campaign in the Mediterranean theater allowed Allied generals to apply their forces most economically and with maximum effect, and thus played a decisive role in shortening the war by mitigating their defeats and accelerating their victories.

## Resistance

Some form of resistance occurred in every country occupied by the Axis, but Yugoslavia is routinely proclaimed as the prime example of the effectiveness of irregular warfare. This is due not only to its mountainous terrain and long coastline, which, with its proximity to Italy, allowed easy access for British Special Operations Executive (SOE) operatives and military supplies, but also to the intense nationalism of Yugoslav national minorities who had a long history of forcibly resisting foreign repression.

Axis occupation of Yugoslavia was, from the beginning, excessively brutal. The first active resistance began almost immediately after the German invasion by the chétniks, a group of Serbian monarchists and mostly former Yugoslav Army officers led by General Dráa Mihailovíc, which operated at least nominally under the command of the Yugoslav government-in-exile. Mihailovíc began receiving SOE assistance in September 1941 for a guerrilla campaign that caused the Germans some discomfort, but his ultimate aim was to rally resistance forces into a Home Army for an uprising to liberate the country from within in coordination with an Allied landing. Mihailovíc was unwilling to embark on large-scale operations until the Germans were weakened by events outside Yugoslavia for fear of mass reprisals and atrocities against Serb civilians. This was an understandable motive since Hitler had developed a simple response to armed revolt, that of executing 100 civilians for every German soldier killed. In the brutal internal war that developed, some 1.4 million people were killed, or about 10 percent of the population, most of whom perished at the hands of their fellow Yugoslavs. The bloodshed was so widespread that Yugoslavia became the most highly devastated region under Axis control outside Poland and the western USSR.

This policy, however, brought Mihailovíc into contact with the communist Partisans led by Josip Bróz, known as Tito, a long-term communist revolutionary who had experienced fighting in the Spanish Civil War. Tito was ultimately fighting for a revolutionary change of power, but he disguised this as a patriotic war against foreign occupation, officially designated the "People's Liberation Struggle," and sought to appeal to all the Yugoslav nationalities. Tito also had no reservations about fighting an unremitting war on the Axis to the bitter end.

The Germans and Italians each sponsored different minority groups, which they cynically exploited in order to divide and rule. Under Axis encouragement, therefore, one of Europe's bloodiest and most brutal civil wars was fought simultaneously with one of its greatest resistance struggles, in addition to endless massacres by the occupying forces and their auxiliaries. In particular the Ustásha, under Ante Pavelíc, in the Independent State of Croatia, inflicted atrocities in a campaign of terror and genocide that were too much even for the SS, but provided rich opportunities for the partisans to recruit. As they became stronger, Tito and Mihailoví became more embroiled in a struggle for the right to organize the post-war state.

As Mihailovíc increasingly concentrated on prosecuting the burgeoning civil war, he made truces with the Italians to acquire weapons and then began collaborating with the Germans also. Tito, meanwhile, was undertaking increasingly ambitious operations against the Germans that threatened their exploitation of the country's mineral resources and their lines of communication with Greece. In May 1943, when the partisans' strength had risen to 20,000, the Germans attacked with a force in excess of 100,000 troops. Tito lost a quarter of his men, which was all the more grievous because the wounded either died or had to be shot until the British instigated a medical airlift to Italy.

Tito's fortunes were dramatically reversed, however, following the Italian capitulation.

He seized large quantities of Italian arms and equipment, as well as recruiting many deserters, which enabled him to train an army of 250,000. The British had been growing progressively disillusioned with Mihailovíc's lackluster results, and when they learned of his collaboration, they switched their allegiance to the partisans, whom they saw as a more skilled and disciplined force. By the end of 1943, the British were convinced that Tito would be much more useful, and he became the recipient of an increasing Anglo-US aid program. The British established a naval and air base on the Yugoslav island of Vis to support partisan operations, and the British Balkan Air Force flew great quantities of arms and equipment to the partisans in the interior of the country. Mihailovíc in Serbia now remained the only obstacle in Tito's path to power. Under the cover of a British-inspired operation to harass the Germans during their evacuation, Tito pushed his way into Serbia and was poised to take control with the arrival of the Red Army.

The principal symbol of Greek resistance was the communist National Liberation Front (EAM), with its military wing, the National People's Liberation Army (ELAS), its rival, the National Republican Greek League (EDES) and other smaller partisan bands, which were unanimously republican. They fought bravely and, with the assistance of British SOE liaison officers, achieved some notable successes. Their most outstanding achievement occurred on November 25–26, 1942, when a joint band of 150 Greeks, coordinated by a British SAS sabotage team, destroyed the Gorgopotamos viaduct, which carried the main Salonika–Athens railway line. It was perhaps the most spectacular act of sabotage in occupied Europe up to that time and disrupted supplies to the Axis forces in north Africa, but it also encouraged each band to continue their separate existence and thus ensured that Greek resistance would not be unified under communist control. From this point forward, relations between the partisans were at best uneasy, but often degenerated into internecine fighting.

The resistance groups were ambivalent about waging war on their occupiers because German reprisals on innocent civilians were extremely severe. Hostages were taken and executed and whole villages wiped out, such as the 1,000 people who were killed in a single incident at Kalavryta. At the Nuremberg war trials after the war, prosecutors testified that in Greece there were a thousand examples of the notorious Lidicé massacre, the Czech village eliminated by the Germans following the assassination of Reinhard Heydrich. In total it is estimated that the German, Italian, and Bulgarian occupiers executed about 113,000 people.

The rival resistance groups were also deeply suspicious of each other, as well as the Greek government-in-exile, the Greek King George II and the British, and were already anticipating the inevitable post-liberation power struggle. This mistrust degenerated into a civil war in the winter of 1943–44 when ELAS attacked the anti-communist partisans. The communists failed to take control, but the British negotiated a political settlement in February 1944. However, following the Italian capitulation in September 1943, Axis control of Greece began to crumble, and through fortune and intrigue, ELAS strengthened their position by securing the arms and equipment of the Italian forces. As a result the communists became the most powerful political and military formation in occupied Greece and simply awaited the end of the war to assume power.

At the conclusion of the war, it was widely accepted that the resistance movements in Greece and Yugoslavia had been a great success, and Tito was credited as being the only leader to have liberated his own country from within. Furthermore, the resistance operations were also judged to have caused the Axis to divert sufficient troops from other theaters and to have materially affected the outcome of the war in those areas. Realistically, it is now recognized that the arrival of the Red Army had much more to do with the liberation of southeastern Europe, while the estimates of the strategic impact on the German war effort are also now accepted as generous.

The occupation troops were principally of Italians, Bulgarians, and Hungarians, as well as Germans. Even after the Italian capitulation, when Hitler had to increase the number of German troops, the German shortage of manpower reduced the forces made available for the Balkan occupation to the overage and the physically limited. With the exception of 1st Mountain Division, which was transferred from Russia in the spring of 1943, few were of sufficient quality for frontline operations against the Allied or Soviet Armies. Other measures taken to alleviate the manpower shortage were the employment of native troops and the enlistment of foreign legionnaires, chiefly Russians and Caucasus Mountain peoples. Of 300 German divisions in 1944, less than 20 were employed in internal security duties. The guerrilla war of sabotage and subversion thus contributed materially little to the ultimate defeat of Nazi Germany, but in Yugoslavia Tito had engineered a national uprising and earned the right to dominate the post-war state.

# A child in the siege of annihilation: Malta 1940–43

## Leon Gambin

A salient characteristic of the campaigns in the Mediterranean was that the fighting was largely conducted in country almost wholly lacking any civilian populations – with one striking exception. Malta is just 117 miles (188 km) square, or about two-thirds the size of the Isle of Wight but, with a population of 270,000 people, it was one of the most densely populated areas in Europe. The island's proximity, just 60 miles (96 km) or 10 minutes' flying time to Sicily, enabled the Axis to inflict an intense bombardment in an attempt to neutralize Malta as an offensive base.

Leon Gambin was a 12-year-old boy living with his family in Senglea, which, together with Vittoriosa and Cospicua, form the Three Cities that lie southeast of Valetta on the opposite side of the Grand Harbor. It bore many traces of the Great Siege of 1565, when an enormous Turkish army was repulsed three times from its ramparts, earning Senglea the proud title "Citta Invicta" – the unconquered city. Amidst narrow, steep roads that were flanked by quaint three-story houses and which ran down to the moats and the harbor, Leon played cheerfully with his four sisters and three brothers. His father owned two shops and the Stoll picture theater, and during the summer operated a kiosk on the quayside where Leon helped out by waiting on the sailors and their girls with ice cream and cool drinks.

This serene atmosphere changed dramatically, however, in June 1940 when Italy declared war. Fearing the bombs, Leon's father squeezed his family into a *Karozzin*, a small traditional Maltese horse-drawn cab, and sent them to safety in the village of Siggiewi, near Rabat. The first bombs had brought nervous reports of death and destruction and, without shelters for protection, almost every family had quickly packed a few essentials and left Senglea to seek refuge in the country, so all that remained in the deserted city were the cats and dogs. Although the island's only defense were the three famous Gladiator biplane fighters *Faith, Hope,* and *Charity,* the Italians were not resolute in their attacks, and the Maltese people could hear the scared Italian pilots on the radio, so during the next six months, Leon, his family, and almost everyone else gradually returned to Senglea.

On January 16, 1941, the Germans launched their first blitz on Malta and dropped not confetti, as the Maltese people said of the Italians when they came to raid, but real, high-caliber bombs. During two hours of constant bombing, Senglea was heavily damaged, and 21 people were killed. Many families had hewn shelters in the soft limestone rock in their cellars and dug tunnels to link with cellars and wells of neighboring families to provide an escape if the entrance was blocked. Leon was safe, although his sister Mary was trapped in the rubble and managed to escape through another well. The bombing also completely destroyed the Basilica of Our Lady of Victory, built to celebrate the victory by the Knights of Malta in 1565, except the crucifix which remained undamaged and stood triumphant above the rubble. The devoutly religious Maltese quickly assessed the significance that, just as the cross had triumphed over the Turks, victory in this siege was equally certain.

Leon's father again took his family to Siggiewi, without knowing where they would live, but the Maltese people showed boundless charity by taking in complete strangers who had fled the city or whose homes had been destroyed. Leon was lucky that his father was a shopkeeper and, using his business acumen,

Malta was one of the most densely populated areas in Europe and suffered the most intense blitz of the war. Civilians suffered terribly as their homes were often near the harbor or military bases, forcing the population to live underground and in near starving conditions. (Imperial War Museum A8613)

opened a shop in Rabat. Known as "Gambin the Confectioner" he sold whatever he could obtain through bartering but especially alcohol and specialist sweet pastries. Rationing first started on April 7, 1941, with sugar, coffee, soap, and matches, but by September that year, almost everything was being rationed. A shortage of coins also made it hard to do business, but a system of IOUs was introduced, and these were used extensively as small change and were routinely honored. The women too had to be equally resourceful, and imaginative improvisation made life a little more bearable. Many women tailored clothes for the children from British service blankets, old tires were used to resole shoes, and almost everything was recycled.

Leon's family were luckier than most in that their home was not demolished. His mother still had a means to prepare food, and through his business and trading

contacts Leon's father was able to provide for his family. The British servicemen stationed on Malta were also restricted to the same rationing that applied to civilians, and hunger was widespread. Although Leon's family had little to share, they were friendly with a few soldiers stationed who frequented their shop, and when times were tough, they would come into the shop and, using a secret code so as not to alert everyone, for the family could help but a few, would leave their beret lying open on a chair. This was a sign for Leon, who would then run to tell his mother "Tom's here, he's left his beret for something to eat." Surreptitiously she would place something, often a well-made Maltese sandwich, in the beret, and the soldier would roll it up and quietly take it with him. With meager food to spare for themselves, these efforts were symbolic of the generosity of the Maltese people toward those helping to defend their island.

The caves and catacombs on the island were not sufficient to provide safety for everyone and, for those not lucky enough to have their own shelters, coal miners serving in the Royal Engineers dug large public shelters. As the blitz worsened, the raids became more frequent, averaging eight or nine per day. The longest single raid lasted 13 hours, and on one day alone, 21 hours were spent under alert. People had to remain underground for hours at a time, and from December 1941, when the bombing intensified, the entire population took to living underground almost permanently. Conditions in the shelters were terrible. Cold, wet, dirty, without proper sanitation, and, with only candles and hurricane lamps to light the dark nights, people relied on their faith to see them through. Many shelters were turned into chapels, and communal prayers were held. Men and women screamed out in panic, fear, and prayer, and it is a commonly held belief that their fervent prayers to let the bombs drop into the sea saved them from death and destruction.

In the lull between raids, life went on as normal. Leon attended Birkirkara St. Aloysius Jesuit College, and, while lessons were conducted as normally as possible, life as a schoolboy was far from normal. To save fuel the bus terminus was moved to the outskirts of each town, which in Rabat meant that Leon and his three friends had to make a scary walk across Ta' Qali airfield each day to catch their bus. The airfield was used by Spitfires and was frequently bombed, so the boys had to scan the skies for enemy aircraft and then either rush across while it was safe or find a stone wall to hide behind or some other secure place until the bombing had finished. Leon made an error only once, judging it safe after school while rushing to the bus stop hoping to catch a ride home,

while two Spitfires were chasing a German fighter. Although not a bomber, in an attempt to evade his pursuers, the German pilot swooped low and released a bomb from under his wings just where Leon was standing. The bomb exploded and showered Leon in dirt, but luckily he remained unhurt.

Free from the confines of the shelter, the children played with extra energy, but theirs was no ordinary playfield. Antipersonnel mines were designed to look like pens, butterflies or cans of sardines and were dropped everywhere. Despite radio warnings not to touch anything strange, children were attracted by such objects and were regularly maimed. Children were prone to find the bomb sites exciting places to play and explore, but regardless of the bombs, the antiaircraft fire was so strong that there was a steady rain of hot, dangerous shrapnel falling from the exploding shells. Leon had a particularly disturbing experience on March 21, 1942, when exploring a bombsite at the Point de Vue Hotel in Rabat. The hotel had been requisitioned as a billet for officers stationed at the nearby Ta' Qali airfield, and Leon was one of the first to discover five pilots who had been decapitated by a bomb, a shocking experience that remains with him today. A sunny Sunday on May 9 proved a much happier day when Leon and his friends were able to sit atop the hill above Ta' Qali airfield and with great joy watch 64 Spitfires land after flying in from the aircraft carriers USS *Wasp* and HMS *Eagle*. They were immediately refueled and rearmed and took off to meet the next German raid with a vengeance.

As food stocks diminished during the summer of 1942, malnutrition spread. The quality of bread deteriorated as it was made with 20 percent potatoes, the firewood for the bakeries ran out, and adults were often restricted to 1,100 calories per day. On May 5, the government took the drastic action of rationing bread to 10 oz (300 g) per person per day. As the deprivation of food and cooking fuel worsened, the government established communal "victory kitchens" for people with no means to cook and to economize. In June 1942 there were 42, but at the peak of the siege, 200 kitchens were operating throughout Malta, and the number of people drawing meals rose to over 100,000 in October 1942, going up to 175,536 in the first week of January 1943.

The victory kitchens were, however, more commonly known as siege kitchens, and provided meager daily sustenance. The fare was less than appetizing, not least because everything was cooked in only one way, by being boiled, and readers often wrote to the editor of *The Times of Malta*. One person complained: "the staple diet included goat's meat which was as tough as hide, with tomato sauce or a couple of beans. Each serving was miserable! Our cook used to mince goat meat and turn it into a meat loaf. That way it was possible to eat it without damaging your teeth." Another reader commented about the *minestra*, a vegetable soup: "the vegetables are cut in big chunks, half a turnip, big pieces of long-marrow with skin, turnip leaves and stalks in quantity, a shadow of pumpkin and tomatoes, just to give a hectic color, a few *zibeg*, a type of pasta, swimming in water ... pure water. Not very inviting."

It is estimated that the Germans dropped 17,000 tons of bombs on Malta and, up to October 8, 1942, 9,000 houses were destroyed and 17,000 seriously damaged. Malta was suffering from an acute shortage of all essentials, and although the people did not lose their nerve, the government had to make provision for "Harvest Day," or "Target Day," the day of reckoning when the suffering Maltese would be forced to capitulate through starvation. On April 15, 1942, King George VI announced: "To honor her brave people, I award the George Cross to the Island Fortress of Malta to bear witness to a heroism and devotion that will long be famous in history." Publicly, the

bestowal of the medal helped to boost the morale of the people, but in Leon's family and thousands of others just like his, all of whom were starving, the cry was, "We want bread, not the George Cross," and anti-British sentiment started to rise.

Malta was saved by the Pedestal convoy, which arrived during August 1942. Just five ships arrived out of the 15 that left England, but each was welcomed with delirious excitement. The tanker *Ohio* was literally carried into Grand Harbor slung between two destroyers and with her decks awash. The fuel and supplies staved off starvation and enabled Malta to remain in the fight, but it did not lift the siege. The harsh rationing and suffering of the Maltese people continued until the beginning of 1943, by which stage the fortune of war in the Mediterranean had swung against the Axis and supply convoys could safely be sent to Malta.

In Maltese history, September 8 is a very significant date as it marks the end of the Great Siege of 1565, but it is also the feast day of Our Lady of Victories, *Il-Festa tal-Bambina*, the titular feast of Senglea. In 1943 it was fitting that a large parade was held to celebrate the return of the statue of Our Lady, *Il-Bambina*, from where it had been taken in January 1941 for safekeeping. This was the first procession since 1939, and many Sengleans, including Leon and his family, cleared the streets of rubble for the parade so that they could celebrate the National day and give thanks for deliverance from three years of onslaught. As the procession reached the devastated wharf, the parish priest announced the joyous news just received by the Admiralty that Italy had surrendered, and ships in the harbor used their searchlights to celebrate the end of the long ordeal suffered by the people of Malta.

# Not necessarily in peace

## The Balkans

During 1944 Churchill became increasingly concerned about the communist tide sweeping across Europe in the wake of the Red Army, and its portent for control of post-war Europe. To prevent the communists taking control of Greece, which he saw as vital to British interests in the Mediterranean, Churchill accordingly made an agreement with Stalin in May 1944 to allow Soviet domination of Romania in return for a free British hand in Greece. In Moscow in October 1944, this deal was widened to include Hungary, Bulgaria, and Yugoslavia when they drew up the spheres of influence that the two countries were to have in the Balkans. Initially these were agreed to be 50:50 for Hungary and Yugoslavia and 75:25 between the USSR and others in Bulgaria, but subsequent haggling produced amended ratios for Hungary and Bulgaria of 80:20 in favor of the USSR.

On August 20, Stalin launched a great offensive on the Ukranian Front to "liberate" southeastern Europe. Romania's capitulation on August 23 allowed the Soviet Army to sweep forward rapidly, capturing the great oil fields at Ploesti on August 30 and Bucharest the next day, and reaching the Yugoslavian border on the Danube on September 6. Bulgaria surrendered without resistance on September 9, and by the end of the month, the entire German Sixth Army, totaling more than 100,000 troops, had been captured. Field-Marshal Maximilian von Weichs, Commander-in-Chief, Southeastern Europe, had 600,000 troops between Trieste and the Aegean Sea, but, as German control of the Balkans began to collapse, their position became untenable. Army Group E began to evacuate the Greek islands from September 12, but when the danger of a new Soviet breakthrough westward from Bulgaria threatened the vital railway through Yugoslavia, they began to withdraw from the whole of Greece on October 12. Their only chance of survival was to retrace the route over which the German Army had advanced with such fanfare in 1941 and link up with Army Group F in Yugoslavia. Relatively peacefully, though harried by partisans and the Bulgarian Army, the last Germans finally quit Greece in the first week of November.

The newly formed Greek government of national unity under Prime Minister George Papandreou, recognized as the legitimate government by the Allies, returned to their homeland on October 18 accompanied by the British expedition to Greece, a military force commanded by Lieutenant-General Ronald Scobie. The communist EAM/ELAS had demanded key positions in the government, but this impasse was resolved by Stalin's agreement with Churchill, and he withdrew Soviet support for the communists. Both main partisan forces agreed to demobilize and place their considerable armed forces under the control of the British, acting as a de facto national army for the government, but tensions remained extremely high. At a mass EAM demonstration on December 3 in Athens, 21 people were shot by police in circumstances that remain unclear even now, but the shooting provoked a communist insurgency and within a few days ELAS, and British troops were locked in bloody street-fighting.

The British sent reinforcements from the campaign in Italy, which they could ill-afford, and after six weeks, vicious fighting quelled the insurrection, at a tragic cost of over 200 British lives. The conflict between the dissident allies was unique in World War II and its acrimony was such that not even Churchill and Eden could negotiate a settlement during an impulsive visit to Athens on Christmas Eve 1944. A cease-fire was achieved in January 1945, and a political settlement negotiated the following month, but the peace that followed proved to be illusory as the communists renewed their bitter struggle 18 months later. The liberation of Greece from the choke of Axis control merely created a vacuum in which the chaos of an acrimonious civil war continued until finally defeated in 1949 by an American-equipped and trained Greek Army, in a prelude to the emerging Cold War. However, the communist atrocities that had accompanied the attempted insurrection left an indelible mark on a whole generation of Greeks that still runs deep in Greek society today.

The sudden appearance of the Red Army on the Yugoslav border prompted Tito to fly to Moscow to meet Stalin. He agreed to allow troops of the 3rd Ukrainian Front to participate in the capture of Belgrade and to arm 14 partisan divisions, which allowed Tito to conquer étnik-dominated Serbia. Stalin also gave the impression that he had "requested" permission to allow the Red Army to cross Yugoslavia in order to shorten its advance for an assault on southern Hungary in exchange for allowing Tito a role in the postwar administration of Yugoslavia. The battle for Belgrade duly began on October 14, and despite a fierce defense by the Germans, who lost 25,000 in casualties, the city fell six days later.

German Army Group F had incorporated Army Group E following its flight from Greece, but the way remained open for the Soviet forces to continue their advance through Yugoslavia. However, Hitler orchestrated a coup in Hungary and declared Budapest to be a fortress, thus ensuring the Soviet advance up the Danube would be a fierce fight. Stalin may also have had in mind his agreement with Churchill, but he ordered that Soviet forces turn back for the coming battle for Hungary. In hindsight the decision to remove Soviet troops from Yugoslavia at the moment of victory proved to be a misjudgment that deprived Stalin of

the ability to impose Soviet rule consistently across the whole of eastern Europe.

Nevertheless, with a force of several hundred thousand well-armed troops now operating as a regular army, Tito was able to continue the task of liberating Yugoslavia as the Germans, and their Yugoslav auxiliaries slowly fell back northward. On March 19, 1945, the Fourth Yugoslav Army launched an offensive that reached Trieste on April 30, but military operations were not concluded until May 15, after the final German surrender. Tito formed an internationally recognized coalition government, under communist control, and began the process of establishing an independent, authoritarian communist regime, of which he became president for life. Despite constant nationalistic, ethnic, and religious tensions, the partisan war of national liberation remained the source of authority and inspiration behind the "brotherhood and unity" that maintained Tito's regime until his death in 1980.

## The end in Italy

A prolonged Allied tactical air interdiction program during the autumn and winter of 1944 had effectively closed the Brenner Pass and created an acute shortage of fuel that drastically reduced the mobility of General Heinrich von Vietinghoff's Army Group C in northern Italy. Although the Germans still had over half a million men in the field, the Allies had been invigorated in both spirit and outlook by substantial reinforcements, including the Brazilian Expeditionary Force and an abundant array of new weapons. On April 9, 1945, after the ground had dried, Alexander launched his spring offensive with Eighth Army attacking through the Argenta Gap. Fifth Army struck on April 15, and just ten days later, both Allied armies met at Finale nell'Emilia, after having surrounded and eliminated the last German forces. The Allies then advanced rapidly northward, the Americans entering Milan on April 29 and the British reaching Trieste on May 2. Fifth Army continued to advance into Austria, linking with US Seventh Army in the Brenner Pass on May 6.

The isolated and hopeless position of German forces had led SS General Karl Wolff, military governor and head of the SS in northern Italy, to initiate background negotiations for a separate surrender as early as February 1945. The talks, facilitated by Allan Dulles, head of the American Office of Strategic Services in Switzerland, held much promise, although they were complicated by mutual suspicion and mistrust. Wolff wished to avoid senseless destruction and loss of life and to repel the spread of communism, as well as ingratiating himself with the West in case of war crimes trials, but for the Allies Wolff offered the prospect of preventing the creation of a Nazi redoubt in the Alps. Himmler checked the talks in April, preventing a conclusion before the Allies' spring offensive, but by April 23, Wolff and Vietinghoff decided to disregard orders from Berlin. Wolff ordered the SS not to resist the Italian partisans on April 25, and an unconditional surrender was signed on April 29, to be effective on May 2, six days before the German surrender in the West. Military success had already assured the Allies of victory, but a smoother and quicker conclusion of the fighting ensured that there was no last-ditch stand by die-hard fascists, and curtailed the loss of life and destruction.

Mussolini also made attempts in the last days to come to terms with the Allies behind the backs of the Germans, but on learning of the Germans' own negotiations, he attempted to flee to Switzerland. He was captured by partisans near Lake Como and was shot on April 28, along with his mistress Clara Petacci and the main fascist leaders. Their bodies were then taken to Milan and suspended upside down from meat hooks for public exhibition in the Piazzale Loreto. This gruesome gesture was the conclusion to 20 years of fascist dictatorship and Mussolini's dream of an Italian Empire spanning the Mediterranean, for which the Italian people had paid dearly in wars that they were neither prepared for nor willing to fight.

Italian civilians line the streets as an American M10 tank destroyer enters Rome. The city fell to the Allies on June 12, 1944. Mussolini was executed on April 28, 1945. (FPG/Hulton Archive/Getty Images)

# The end of empire

## The war experience

The Mediterranean theater varied in importance as World War II progressed. Before the entry of Italy in June 1940 it was inactive; from that time onward, until the German attack on the Soviet Union in June 1941, it was the main operational area and the only one where there was fighting on land. It assumed increasing significance, especially after the Anglo-American landings in French northwest Africa in November 1942, until August 1943 when plans for the cross-channel invasion of Europe were approved. However, after Operation Overlord was mounted in June 1944, the Mediterranean became a secondary theater.

In achieving the final defeat of Nazi Germany, the campaigns in the Mediterranean had a subordinate role. The number of troops involved was a minuscule proportion of the armies raised by the Axis and Allied nations. At El Alamein, for example, about 12 Axis divisions faced 13 British divisions, and in Italy, the Allied armies at their maximum strength reached some 20 divisions to face up to 25 German divisions. By comparison, at the height of the war in Europe in 1944, some 300 Axis divisions fought 300 Russian and 70 British and American divisions. The casualties suffered were still significant, though correspondingly lower than other regions of the war, and are notoriously inaccurate, but it is estimated that Allied losses were 180,000 British, 136,000 Americans, 65,000 New Zealanders (including many captured in Greece and Crete), 45,000 French, 22,000 Southern Africans, 21,000 Australians, 12,000 Poles, 2,000 Brazilians, and about 100,000 Greeks, while Axis losses were 768,000 Germans and 623,000 Italians, many of whom were captured in east Africa, the Western Desert, and Tunisia.

Allied victory in the naval war fought in the Mediterranean between June 1940 and September 1943 was hard won. The Italian Navy certainly did not win the war, and ended it by surrendering its ships to the Allies at Malta as part of the armistice. However, contrary to common belief, the Italian Navy was far from inept. Italian sailors succeeded in maintaining the supply routes to Africa and the Balkans, and sank more British ships than they lost. The Italians lost 1,278 merchant ships totaling 2,272,607 tons and 339 naval ships totaling 314,298 tons, including 11 cruisers, 34 destroyers, and 65 submarines. In comparison the British lost 238 naval ships totaling 411,935 tons, including a battleship, two aircraft carriers, 13 cruisers, one monitor, 56 destroyers, and 41 submarines.

Although the fighting in the Mediterranean theater did not materially contribute to the defeat of the Axis armies, it was the decisive training ground for British and American forces. It allowed expertise to be developed in infantry tactics, air and ground operations support, combined arms and amphibious operations, as well as allowing the new allies time to work out unity-of-command issues before the Allied armies undertook the massive challenge of launching a cross-channel invasion of Europe. The powerful military organization of the Grand Alliance that proved so effective in operations against the Germans in Europe was forged in the Mediterranean.

## Decolonization

There is no obvious reason why a war between European powers should be fought in Africa and the Middle East, but World War II spread to this area simply because the

British and the Italians were already there. The British had established an imperial presence some 60 years earlier, and the Italians had belatedly attempted to find their own place in the sun by establishing a colony in Africa. The French too had an empire, based on their control of Algeria and the Levant, so that the entire southern shore of the Mediterranean Sea from the Atlantic Ocean to the Red Sea was under European dominion. Germany became involved only to save its Italian ally and, as a result, in this arena the European nations fought an essentially European war.

But the campaigns in the Mediterranean and Middle East were fought against a background of conflict between colonial ruler and subject, between imperial power and nationalist aspirations, and between Arab and Jew. While the war years themselves saw a remarkable resurgence of confidence in the imperial structure and the strength of colonial ties, World War II acted as a trigger for the forces of anti-imperialism that exploded with ferocity in the decades after the war and led to the rapid unwinding of the colonial system. Although only a relatively small part of Africa had been directly touched by the fighting, the economic and social impact of World War II dramatically affected the African continent. There had been just three truly independent countries in Africa before the war, but with the dissolution of the European empires, a wave of decolonization spread rapidly across the continent, and within just 30 years of the end of the war, all of Africa consisted of independent sovereign states. In the Middle East, the internal politics and society of the colonized areas were affected equally dramatically by the war but with even more profound consequences.

## The Italian Empire

Italy had borne the main cost of the war in the Mediterranean but had, in the year before the war ended, already begun the move toward a new status as a modern, liberal society with functioning democratic institutions, a new role in Europe, and a modernized economy. Relief from the financial burden of the empire, which had always been a drain on the country's slender resources, boosted the domestic economy, but the disposition of Italy's colonies was a question that had to be considered before the peace treaty officially ending the war with Italy was signed in February 1947. Italy renounced all claims to its possessions, but the treaty was vague, stating only that these territories should "remain in their present state until their future is decided." The US, Britain, France, and the Soviet Union took over responsibility for the colonies and established the Four Power Inquiry Commission, but failed to reach agreement on their future and so, in September 1948, referred the matter to the General Assembly of the United Nations.

In Libya, British and French authorities had taken over the civil administration when the fighting had finished. This situation continued in the immediate postwar period as British, French, and Italian administrators established a civil framework and trained local officials, but there was a general international commitment to finding an acceptable system of independent government. In 1949 a UN resolution approved a federal system of government with a monarch, which became effective on December 24, 1951, when King Idris I proclaimed the independence of the United Kingdom of Libya as a sovereign state.

The decolonization of the fascist empire took place when the colonial powers were still strong, in contrast to the liberation of most other European colonies two decades later. The latter were liberated as single units while the liberation of Italian East Africa, which the fascists had ruled as a single entity, was, on the contrary, effected piecemeal, and resulted in the fragmentation of the territory once more into three political entities: Ethiopia, Eritrea, and Somalia. Each emerged to independence separately, and at a different time, which militated against the maintenance of regional unity that the Italians had established.

During the war in Ethiopia, British military officials left responsibility for internal affairs in the hands of Emperor Haile Selassie, and an interim Anglo-Ethiopian arrangement in January 1942 confirmed Ethiopia's status as a sovereign state. About the same time, a US economic mission arrived, thereby laying the groundwork for an alliance that in time would significantly affect the country's direction. After the post-war relationship with Britain wound down in 1952, in keeping with a 1950 UN resolution, the emperor asked the US for military assistance and economic support, increasing his dependence on Washington. Despite his many years as emperor and his international stature, however, there was almost no significant section of the Ethiopian population on which Haile Selassie could rely to support him in his efforts at economic, social, and political reform. A failed coup d'etat in 1960 heralded a period of frequently violent agitation to confront land reform, corruption, and famine that culminated in a military coup in 1974, in which the aging emperor was arrested and imprisoned.

Eritrea was placed under separate British military administration in 1941, but the first settlement providing an autonomous Eritrean Assembly and Constitution did not occur until September 1952. The UN resolved that Eritrea should be linked to Ethiopia through a loose federal structure under the sovereignty of the Ethiopian crown but with a form and organization of internal self-government. Almost from the start of the federation, however, the emperor's representative undercut the territory's separate status under the federal system. In November 1962, the Eritrean Assembly voted unanimously, amidst allegations of bribery, to change Eritrea's status to that of a province of Ethiopia, but the extinction of the federation consolidated internal and external opposition to union. Beginning in 1961, the opposition turned to armed struggle and, by 1966, challenged imperial forces throughout Eritrea, intensifying the internecine guerrilla war.

The British military government in Italian Somaliland departed on April 1, 1950, when the country became a UN trust territory under Italian administration and was renamed Somalia. Independence was granted on July 1, 1960, when Somalia merged with the former British protectorate of Somaliland to form the Somali Democratic Republic. However, no clear legal border was agreed with Ethiopia, and the twin evils of war and famine that grew out of the negligent and corrupt Italian east Africa soon began to flourish. A coup d'etat in 1969 augured the creation of a socialist state under a Supreme Revolutionary Council, and following a severe drought in 1974, Somalia began its descent into anarchy.

# The French Empire

## Northwest Africa

After the fall of the Algerian Vichy regime, Muslim opinions hardened against deep-rooted French colonial attitudes, and an increasing number of nationalists called for armed revolution. Tensions between the Muslim and Colon communities exploded on May 8, 1945, V-E Day, during demonstrations calling for Algerian liberation, in which 103 Europeans were killed. Postwar elections were blatantly rigged, and Colon extremists took every opportunity to persuade the French government of the need for draconian measures against the emergent independence movement.

On November 1, 1954, the National Liberation Army (ALN), the military arm of the National Liberation Front (FLN), began the Algerian War of Independence with a number of guerrilla attacks. In response, the French government declared that the Algerian *départements* were part of the French Republic and that there could be no conceivable secession, and sent 400,000 troops to put down the uprising. The populist guerrilla war paralyzed Algeria and the brutal methods used by the French forces, including torture, turned world opinion against France. The French government was caught between a colonial policy based on racism and exploitation, which elicited invidious comparisons with totalitarian regimes and Nazism, and its place as a standard-bearer of democracy.

Recurrent cabinet crises focused attention on the inherent instability of the Fourth Republic, and the feeling was widespread that another debacle like that of Indochina in 1954 was in the offing. Many saw Charles de Gaulle, who had not held office since 1946, as the only public figure capable of rallying the nation and preserving French Algeria, and in 1958, French army commanders staged a coup d'etat.

De Gaulle became premier with the support of the political extreme right and was given carte blanche to deal with Algeria. The French army won military control in 1958–59, but de Gaulle announced a referendum for Algerian self-determination. The Colons and units of the French army saw this as a betrayal and staged unsuccessful insurrections in January 1960 and April 1961, but the "generals' putsch" marked the turning point in the official attitude toward the Algerian war. A cease-fire was announced in March 1962, and despite a ruthless terrorist campaign by Colon vigilantes, a referendum was held in July.

Nearly eight years of revolution and 42,000 recorded terrorist incidents had cost the lives of up to a million people from war-related causes, but the Democratic and Popular Republic of Algeria was formally proclaimed at the opening session of the National Assembly on September 25, 1962. Within a year, 1.4 million refugees, including almost the entire Jewish community and some pro-French Muslims, had joined the exodus to France. Fewer than 30,000 Europeans chose to remain in Algeria.

Following the Axis surrender in 1943, control of Tunisia was handed over to the Free French, and the reigning *bey* was arrested as a German collaborator, which triggered nationalist unrest. Violent resistance to French rule erupted in 1954, and France promised the protectorate full internal autonomy under a Tunisian government. In March 1956, the French recognized Tunisia as a sovereign state, ruled as a constitutional

monarchy under the *bey*, but the following year, Tunisia was proclaimed a republic, and many French residents fled. Relations with France deteriorated still further in 1957 when Tunisian and French troops clashed along the Algerian border, and Tunisia demanded the French evacuate a naval base at Bizerte, which Tunisian troops held under siege in July 1961. After UN intervention, France finally withdrew from Tunisia in October 1963.

In Morocco, King Mohammed V first demanded independence in January 1944 after the defeat of the Vichy regime, and revived resistance to foreign occupation in 1947. His exile in 1953 sparked a revolution, but without the violence that occurred in Algeria or even Tunisia, and in 1956, France recognized the independence of the Kingdom of Morocco.

## Syria and Lebanon

The promise made by the British and the Free French during the capture of Syria and Lebanon in 1941 to honor their independence precluded any return to French rule, either directly or by mandate. In 1943, new independent governments were elected, and in 1944, the Soviet Union and the US granted Syria and Lebanon unconditional recognition as sovereign states; British recognition followed a year later. Anglo-US pressure forced the French to concede real powers to the indigenous governments, but France attempted to secure special cultural, economic, and strategic privileges in Syria before agreeing to withdraw. Syrian opposition culminated in May 1945 when demonstrations occurred in Damascus and Aleppo and, for the third time in 20 years, the French bombed and machine-gunned the ancient capital. De Gaulle ordered a cease-fire, but only after Churchill threatened to send British troops to Damascus to intervene. The French acceded to a UN resolution in February 1946 calling for a withdrawal, and by April 15, all French troops were off Syrian soil. Even de Gaulle was forced to accept that defeat in 1940 had cost France its position in the

Levant. When the British left Syria in 1946, the country became a republic, but political instability followed with one military coup after another.

For a while after 1943, independent Lebanon was a model ecumenical society. Its strategic location and relatively stable government made it a major trade and financial center. But an unbalanced power-sharing arrangement and the rise of the Arab–Israeli conflict, which Lebanon was gradually drawn into, were fatal flaws that marred the country's chance for lasting peace.

# The British Empire

## Iraq and Iran

With the end of the war, the rationale for the occupation of Iraq and Iran had ended. Britain evacuated Iran in keeping with the tripartite treaty of alliance signed in January 1942, under which Britain and the Soviet Union agreed to respect Iran's independence and territorial integrity, and to withdraw their troops from Iran within six months of the end of hostilities. Soviet troops, however, remained in Iran to pressure the government for oil concessions by supporting autonomous Azarbaijan and Kurdish Republics, and were evacuated reluctantly only after intense US, British, and UN pressure. In 1947, Iran and the United States signed an agreement providing military aid to support the Shah and his pro-Western government, while in Iraq the British maintained their influence through the new young King Faisal II as various pro-Western pacts were signed.

Both countries continued their tortuous path to full independence, but the bitterness that had been engendered between the military occupiers, colonial rulers, pro-British politicians, the monarchy, and Islamic nationalists continued in the postwar world. The bitter opposition to union with the West, exemplified in a series of uprisings and attempted coups d'etat that included the 1941 Rashid Ali movement, came to a climax in

Baghdad in 1958 when the Hashimite monarchy was overthrown in a military coup and Iraq was proclaimed a republic, all of which in turn led to the ongoing troublesome relationship with the United States.

## Egypt and Sudan

Unfettered control had enabled Britain to turn Egypt into a massive military depot, from which the war in the Mediterranean was won, but the social and political consequences were, therefore, far more profound. Relations between the British and Egyptians had always been strained, but under the pressure of wartime conditions, and with an enlarged military population, anti-British sentiment became more volatile. When, in February 1942, the pro-British government resigned following popular demonstrations in favor of Rommel, King Farouk refused to comply with a directive from the British ambassador, Sir Miles Lampson, to abdicate or appoint a pro-British government led by Mustafa al-Nahhas, head of the Wafd, an upper-class nationalist movement. Almost immediately British armored cars and infantry surrounded the Abdin Palace, and King Farouk was browbeaten into yielding to the British demand. In turn the King was obliged to keep the pro-British Nahhas government in office until nearly the end of the war.

King Farouk resented continued British dominance, but some of the extremist nationalist officers in the Egyptian Army, such as Gamal Abd el-Nasser and Anwar Sadat, were in touch with the Germans, without understanding that Axis occupation would be far more oppressive than the British. The officers were arrested, and by its show of power, Britain secured its base for the decisive campaigns during 1942. However, the underlying effect was to humiliate the royal house, on which the British had long relied for access to the political process, while the imperial domination exacerbated Egyptian antagonism toward the British, exhausting the last vestiges of their support. This episode left a bitter legacy that contributed

## Compass and Rommel (1)

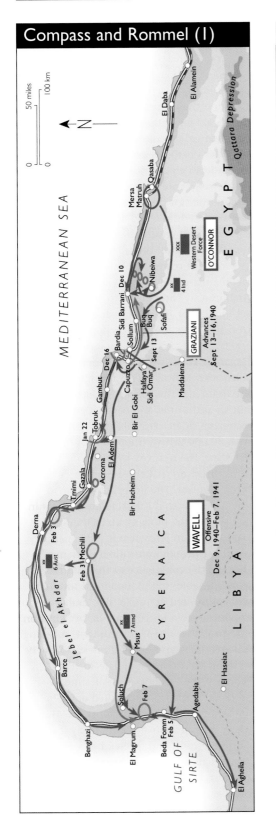

## Compass and Rommel (2)

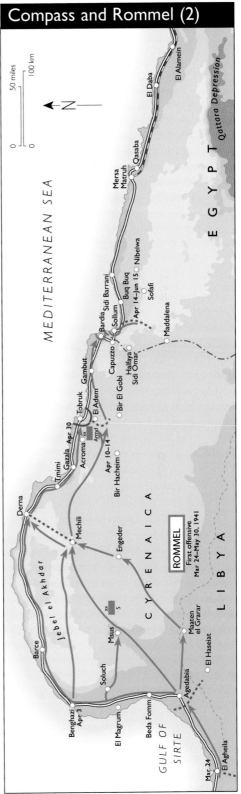

to the animosity during the Suez crisis, just over a decade later.

As the war moved away from Egypt, the domestic situation diminished in importance to the British and to the overall war effort, and the rise of Egyptian nationalism became more serious. With the threat to the Suez Canal removed, the Wafd called for the immediate evacuation of British troops from Egypt, but the British were slow to respond and Egyptian resentment exploded in anti-British riots and strikes. Under pressure from the Wafd and the highly organized Muslim Brotherhood, which had grown in power and influence during the war years, British troops were evacuated from Alexandria in 1947, and the headquarters of the Middle East command was transferred to Cyprus.

The Wafd blocked British attempts to renegotiate the Anglo-Egyptian Alliance, and when Nahhas became prime minister in 1952, he repealed the 1936 treaty that had given Britain the right to control the Suez Canal. His dismissal by King Farouk ignited anti-British riots that were put down by the army, which in turn compelled a group of army officers, led by Nasser, to stage a coup d'etat. King Farouk was forced to abdicate, all political parties were banned, the Constitution was nullified, and in 1953, the Egyptian Arab Republic was declared. The following year, the British finally left Egypt.

Britain retained control of the Sudan, despite growing demands by the Egyptians for British withdrawal, and in 1953, the two governments agreed to allow a three-year transitional period leading to total Sudanese independence. The first Sudanese elections were held late in 1953, and the first all-Sudanese government took office in 1954, when the new Republic of the Sudan was born.

## Palestine

In May 1939, Britain adopted a pro-Arab stance to secure its position in Palestine and the Middle East, and consolidated its hold in 1941 by removing French imperial interests and thwarting German attempts to exert control, all of which saved the British Empire in the Middle East during the war – but not beyond. The British also worked with the Jewish Agency, a Jewish quasi-government that contributed much materiel to the British war effort. Although the Zionists favored the establishment of a Jewish national home in Palestine, they refrained from harassing the British so long as the war lasted, but they in turn resorted to violence when the war ended.

Hitler's barbarous treatment of the Jews engendered a powerful Jewish nationalism and a passionate desire within the Jewish community for the immediate creation of a Jewish state that could accommodate the survivors and ensure that there was a haven for all Jews for all time. The British government controlled Palestine under a UN mandate, but, fearful of fermenting Arab unrest, had refused to amend the limit set in 1939 of 75,000 Jewish immigrants over five years, despite US pressure to admit 100,000 survivors of the Holocaust. Haganah, the semi-official Zionist militia, sided with radical Jewish terrorists such as the Irgun and the Stern gang against the British authorities and began a guerrilla campaign in October 1945. By spring 1946, with 80,000 British troops deployed in Palestine, the territory trembled on the edge of insurrection that threatened to develop into open war. The British government attempted to keep Palestine peaceful, and British, but the blowing up of the King David Hotel in Jerusalem in July 1946, in which 91 people were killed, particularly shocked the conscience of the civilized world. Unable to find a political solution and confronted by implacable Arab opposition to a Jewish state of any kind in Palestine, the British government, suffering war-weariness and under domestic pressure to bring the troops home, decided in February 1947 to refer the Palestine problem to the UN and pulled out. The Jews then took up arms against the Arabs, who came up against them jointly if not in a unified front, and evicted half of the Palestinian population through violence and fear. On May 14, 1948, the state of Israel was proclaimed and a new chapter in Middle Eastern history was opened.

# Conclusion

World War I caused the collapse of Turkish Ottoman rule. Instead of satisfying the ambition of an Arabia for the Arabs, however, the French and British victors selected the choicest regions and simply replaced that rule of one empire with the rule of another. World War II was also a European war that was fought out on the tableau of Middle Eastern national aspirations, but victory left a political vacuum. Early defeat of the French eliminated it as a first-ranked power, and the internecine struggles to hold on to its colonial vestiges left such a bad taste that its empire was lost. The British had fought a bitter struggle to the very end and lacked the heart to continue fighting for something to which they themselves felt they no longer had the right.

Moreover, the global political situation had changed. In the Atlantic Charter, announced in August 1941, Britain and the US had asserted that one of the principles for which they would fight fascist despotism was "the right of all peoples to choose the form of government under which they will live." This noble declaration gave a legitimacy to the forces of anti-imperialism but the major victors, the US and Soviet Union, were themselves implacably opposed to European colonialism.

The establishment of the UN, in part to ensure a more equitable world order, also gave an impetus to the process of decolonization. In the Mediterranean and the Middle East, therefore, new opportunities were created for Arabs that coincided with the swelling nationalist and revolutionary currents in the Arab world. But World War II introduced a new check on Arab ambitions in the form of Zionism and the creation of the State of Israel. By galvanizing and brutalizing the Zionist movement, it is ironic that in their own perverted way Hitler and the Nazis probably did more for Zionism than any Jewish leader.

The Mediterranean and the Middle East region nevertheless remains what it has been for centuries – one of the world's most convenient arteries for travel and commerce – and in the twentieth century it became one of the world's primary sources of oil wealth. For these reasons the rest of the world maintains its interests there, and, although the interests have taken on a new guise, the region remains as unsettled as ever.

## Crusader (1)

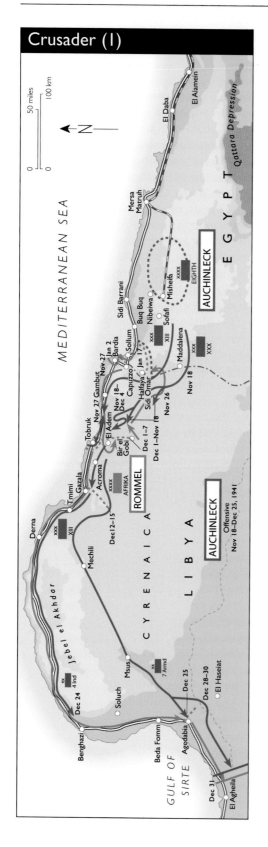

## Crusader (2)

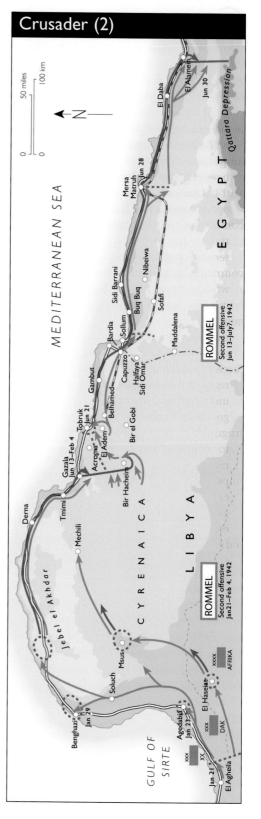

# Glossary

**aerodrome** An airfield, or any location from which aircraft flight operations take place.

**amphibious warfare** Warfare carried out on both land and in water.

**anti-bolshevism** Political and ideological opposition to communism.

**commerce** A division of trade or production that deals with the exchange of goods and services from producer to final consumer.

**communist** A totalitarian government in which a single party controls state-owned means of production.

**empire** A geographically extensive group of states and peoples, united and ruled by an emperor or oligarchy.

**fascist** A political philosophy, movement, or regime that puts the nation before the individual and stands for a centralized government headed by a dictator.

**frogmen** Military personnel who are trained to dive or swim for the purpose of reconnaissance and demolition.

**imperialism** The policy or practice of extending the power of a nation by gaining control over the political or economic life of other areas.

**industrialization** A process of social and economic change that grows through technological advancement.

**infantry** Soldiers specifically trained to fight on foot.

**militarism** The belief of a government or people that a country should maintain a strong military capability and be prepared to use it to defend or promote national interests.

**nationalism** Loyalty or devotion to one nation above all others, placing primary emphasis on promotion of its culture and interests, as opposed to those of other nations.

**pacifist** Someone who opposes war or violence as a means of settling disputes or gaining advantage.

**partisan** One expressing allegiance to one party, faction, cause or person.

**propaganda** The spreading of ideas, information, or rumor for the purpose of helping or injuring an institution, cause, or person.

**protectorate** The relationship of superior authority assumed by one power or state over a dependent one.

**quagmire** A soft, often messy area that is difficult to maneuver through.

**repercussions** An action or effect given or exerted in return.

**schism** A formal division or split.

# For More Information

**Franklin D. Roosevelt Presidential Library and Museum**
4079 Albany Post Road
Hyde Park, NY 12538
(800) FDR-VISIT (337-84748)
Web site: http://www.fdrlibrary.marist.edu
Roosevelt's library and museum houses a collection of historical papers, books, and memorabilia.

**Holocaust Memorial Resource and Education Center of Florida**
851 North Maitland Avenue
Maitland, FL 32751
(407) 628-0555
Web site: http://www.holocaustedu.org
This center is dedicated to using the history and lessons of the holocaust to build a more just and caring community, free of racism and bigotry.

**Imperial War Museum London**
Lambeth Road
London SE1 6HZ
United Kingdom
+44 (0)20 7416 5374
Web site: http://www.iwm.org.uk
This multibranched national museum was founded in 1917 to collect and record artifacts from World Wars I and II.

**National World War II Museum**
945 Magazine Street
New Orleans, LA 70130
(504) 527-6012
Web site:
http://www.nationalww2museum.org
This New Orleans museum houses artifacts and exhibits from World War II.

**U.S. Holocaust Memorial Museum**
100 Raoul Wallenberg Place SW
Washington, DC 20024
(202) 488-0400
Web site: http://www.ushmm.org
This living memorial to the Holocaust works against genocide in modern times as well.

**Winston Churchill Memorial and Library**
Westminster College
501 Westminster Avenue
Fulton, MO 65251
(573) 592-5369
Web site: http://www.churchillmemorial.org
This museum and memorial is located at the site of Churchill's famous "Iron Curtain" speech.

**Web Sites**
Due to the changing nature of Internet links, Rosen Publishing has developed an online list of Web sites related to the subject of this book. This site is updated regularly. Please use this link to access this list:

http://www.rosenlinks.com/wweh/medi

# For Further Reading

Adams, Simon. *World War II*. New York, NY: DK, 2007.

Bosworth, R. J. B. *Mussolini's Italy: Life Under the Fascist Dictatorship, 1915–1945*. New York, NY: Penguin, 2007.

Gilbert, Sir Martin. *The Second World War: A Complete History*. New York, NY: Holt, 2004.

Gooch, John. *Mussolini and His Generals: The Armed Forces and Fascist Foreign Policy 1922–1940*. New York, NY: Cambridge, 2007.

Hibbert, Christopher. *Mussolini: The Rise and Fall of Il Duce*. New York, NY: Palgrave Macmillan, 2008.

Keegan, John. *The Second World War*. New York, NY: Penguin, 2005.

Kershaw, Ian. *Hitler: A Biography*. New York, NY: W. W. Norton, 2008.

Kershaw, Ian. *Hitler, the Germans, and the Final Solution*. New Haven, CT: Yale University Press, 2009.

Mazower, Mark. *Hitler's Empire: How the Nazis Ruled Europe*. New York, NY: Penguin, 2008.

Morris, Rob. *Untold Valor: Forgotten Stories of American Bomber Crews Over Europe in World War II*. Dulles, VA: Potomac, 2006.

Moseley, Ray. *Mussolini: The Last 600 Days of Il Duce*. Lanham, MD: Rowman & Littlefield, 2004.

Porch, Douglas. *The Path to Victory: The Mediterranean Theater in World War II*. Old Saybrook, CT: Konecky and Konecky, 2008.

Ramsden, John. *Man of the Century: Winston Churchill and His Legend Since 1945*. New York, NY: Cambridge, 2003.

Smith, Jean Edward. *FDR*. New York, NY: Random House, 2008.

Wagner, Margaret E., Linda Barrett Osborne, and Susan Reyburn. *The Library of Congress World War II Companion*. New York, NY: Simon & Schuster, 2007.

# Bibliography

## Official histories

Bharucha, P. C. *Official History of Indian Armed Forces in the Second World War: North African Campaign, 1940–1943*, Delhi, 1956.

Deist, Wilhelm, et al. "The Mediterranean, South-East Europe and North Africa 1939–1941" in *Germany and the Second World War*, Oxford, 1990.

Gill, G. Hermon. "Royal Australian Navy, 1939–1942" in *Australia in the War of 1939–1945*, Canberra, 1957.

Hellenic Army General Staff. *Abridged History of the Greek-Italian and Greek-German War*, Athens, 1997.

Herington, John. "Air War Against Germany and Italy, 1939–1943" in *Australia in the War of 1939–1945*, Canberra, 1954.

Hinsley, F. H. et al. *British Intelligence in the Second World War*, 5 volumes, London, 1981–1990.

Italy, Esercito, Corpo di Stato Maggiore. *Ufficio Storico*, 27 volumes, Rome, 1946–1988.

Italy, Marina Militare, Ufficio Storico. *La Marina Italiana Nella Seconda Guerra Mondiale*, 22 volumes, Rome 1952–1978.

Long, Gavin. "Greece, Crete, and Syria" in *Australia in the War of 1939–1945*, Canberra, 1953.

Long, Gavin. "To Benghazi" in *Australia in the War of 1939–1945*, Canberra, 1961.

Maughan, Barton. "Tobruk and El Alamein" in *Australia in the War of 1939–1945*, Canberra, 1966.

Morison, Samuel Eliot. *History of United States Naval Operations in World War II: Operations in North African Waters*, Boston, 1984.

Morison, Samuel Eliot. *History of United States Naval Operations in World War II: Sicily–Salerno–Anzio*, Boston, 1954

New Zealand War History Branch. *Official History of New Zealand in the Second World War, 1939–1945*, 24 volumes, Wellington, 1952–1987.

Pal, Dharm. *Official History of Indian Armed Forces in the Second World War: Campaign in Italy, 1943–45*, Delhi, 1960.

Playfair, I. S. O. (ed.) et al. *The Official History of the Second World War: The Mediterranean and the Middle East*, 6 volumes, London, 1954–1988.

Prasad, Bisheshwar. *Official History of Indian Armed Forces in the Second World War: East African Campaign, 1940–41*, Delhi, 1963.

South African War Histories Committee. *The South African Forces in World War II*, 11 Volumes, Cape Town, 1952–1982.

US Army. *United States Army in World War II: Mediterranean Theater of Operations*, 4 volumes, Washington DC, 1984–1981.

## Secondary texts

Barker, Elisabeth. *British Policy in Southeast Europe in the Second World War*, London, 1976.

Barnett, Correlli. *The Desert Generals*, London, 1960.

Barnett, Correlli. *Engage the Enemy More Closely*, New York, 1991.

Baynes, John. *The Forgotten Victor, General Sir Richard O'Connor*, London, 1989.

Behrendt, Hans-Otto. *Rommel's Intelligence in the Desert Campaign 1941–1943*, London, 1985.

Belot, Raymond de. *The Struggle for the Mediterranean*, Princeton, 1951.

Bennett, Ralph. *Ultra and the Mediterranean Strategy 1941–1945*, London, 1989.

Bergot, Erwan. *The Afrika Korps*, London, 1976.

Bimberg, Edward L. *Tricolor Over the Sahara: The Desert Battles of the Free French, 1940–1942*, Westport, 2002.

Blaxland, Gregory. *Plain Cook and the Great Showman: First and Eighth Armies in North Africa*, London, 1977.

Bradford, Ernle. *Siege: Malta 1940–1943*, London, 1985.

Bragadin, Marc' Antonio. *The Italian Navy in World War II*, Maryland, 1957.

Breuer, William B. *Operation Torch: The Allied Gamble to Invade North Africa*, New York, 1985.

Buckley, Christopher. *Five Ventures: Iraq-Syria-Persia-Madagascar-Dodecanese*, London, 1977.

Cameron, Ian., *Red Duster, White Ensign: Story of the Malta Convoys*, Garden City, 1959.

Carrell, Paul. *Foxes of the Desert*, Atglen, 1994.

Carver, Michael. *The War in Italy 1939–1945*, London, 2001.

Cervi, Mario. *The Hollow Legions*, New York, 1971.

Coffey, Thomas M. *Lion by the Tail*, New York, 1974.

Connell, John. *Auchinleck*, London, 1959.

Connell, John. *Wavell: Scholar and Soldier*, New York, 1964.

Cunningham, Admiral Andrew B. *A Sailors' Odyssey*, London, 1951.

D'Este, Carlo. *Bitter Victory: The Battle for Sicily, 1943*, New York, 1988.

D'Este, Carlo. *Eisenhower: A Soldier's Story*, New York, 2002.

D'Este, Carlo. *Fatal Decision: Anzio and the Battle for Rome*, New York, 1991.

D'Este, Carlo. *Patton: A Genius for War*, New York, 1995.

D'Este, Carlo. *World War II in the Mediterranean, 1942–1945*, Chapel Hill, 1990.

Dulles, Allen. *Secret Surrender*, New York, 1966.

Foot, M. R. D. *Resistance: European Resistance to Nazism, 1940–1945*, New York, 1977.

Fraser, David. *Knights' Cross*, London, 1993.

Glover, Michael. *Improvised War: The Abyssinian Campaign of 1940–1941*, London, 1987.

Gooch, John. *Italy and the Second World War*, London, 2001.

Greene, Jack, and Alessandro Massignani. *Naval War in the Mediterranean, 1940–1943*, Annapolis, 2002.

Greiffenberg, Hans von. *Partisan Warfare in the Balkans*, Ft Bragg, 1952.

Hamilton, Nigel. *Monty, Master of the Battlefield 1942–1944*, London, 1983.

Harrison, Frank. *Tobruk: The Great Siege Reassessed*, London, 1999.

Haupt, Werner. *The North African Campaign, 1940–1943*, London, 1969.

Heckman, Wolf. *Rommel's War in Africa*, New York, 1995.

Hirszowicz, Lukasz. *The Third Reich and the Arab East*, London, 1966.

Howard, Michael. *The Mediterranean Strategy in the Second World War*, London, 1968.

Irving, David. *The Trail of the Fox*, London, 1977.

Jackson, W. G. F. *The North African Campaign 1940–1943*, London, 1975.

Kelly, Orr. *Meeting the Fox: The Allied Invasion of Africa, from Operation Torch to Kasserine Pass to Victory in Tunisia*, New York, 2002.

Kennedy Shaw, W. B. *Long Range Desert Group*, London, 2000.

Kesselring, Albert. *Memoirs of Field Marshal Kesselring*, Novato, 1989.

Kirk, George. *The Middle East in the War*, London, 1952.

Knox, MacGregor. *Mussolini Unleashed, 1939–1941*, Cambridge, 1982.

Latimer, Jon. *Alamein*, London, 2002.

Levine, Alan J. *War Against Rommel's Supply Lines, 1942–1943*, Westport, 1999.

Lewin, Ronald. *The Chief*, London, 1980.

Liddell Hart, B. H. (ed.). *The Rommel Papers*, London, 1953.

Lind, Lew. *Battle of the Wine Dark Sea: The Aegean Sea Campaign, 1940–1945*, Kenthurst, 1994.

Macintyre, Donald. *Battle for the Mediterranean*, New York, 1964.

Macksey, Kenneth. *Crucible of Power: The Fight for Tunisia 1942–1943*, London, 1969.

Majdalany, Fred. *Cassino: Portrait of a Battle*, London, 1999.

Messenger, Charles. *Tunisian Campaign*, London, 1982.

Mitcham, Samuel W. and Friedrich von Stauffenberg. *The Battle of Sicily*, New York, 1991.

Mockler, Anthony. *Haile Selassie's War: The Italian-Ethiopian Campaign, 1935–1941*, New York, 1984.

Mockler, Anthony. *Our Enemies the French*, London, 1976.

Montagu, Ewan. *The Man Who Never Was*, Oxford, 2001.

Moorehead, Alan. *Desert War: The North African Campaign 1940–1943*, London, 2001.

Osborne, Richard E. *World War II in Colonial Africa: The Death Knell of Colonialism*, Indianapolis, 2001.

Owen, David Lloyd. *Long Range Desert Group, 1940–1945: Providence Their Guide*, Barnsley, 2001.

Pitt, Barrie. *The Crucible of War: Western Desert 1941*, London, 1980.

Pitt, Barrie. *The Crucible of War: Year of Alamein 1942*, London, 1982.

Roberts, Walter R. *Tito, Mihailovic, and the Allies: 1941–1945*, New Brunswick, 1973.

Rolf, David. *Bloody Road to Tunis: Destruction of the Axis Forces in North Africa, November 1942–May 1943*, Mechanicsburg, 2001.

Sadkovich, James J. *The Italian Navy in World War II*, Westport, 1994.

Sandford, Kenneth. *The Mark of the Lion: Charles Upham*, Auckland, 1963.

Schmidt, Heinz Werner. *With Rommel in the Desert*, London, 1997.

Shores, Christopher. *Dust Clouds in the Middle East*, London, 1996.

Smith, E. D. *Victory of a Sort: The British in Greece, 1941–1946*, London, 1988.

Smith, Peter C. *Pedestal: The Convoy That Saved Malta*, Manchester, 1999.

Spooner, Tony. *Supreme Gallantry: Malta's Role in the Allied Victory, 1939–1945*, London, 1996.

Stewart, Richard A. *Sunrise at Abadan: The British and Soviet Invasion of Iran, 1941*, Westport, 1988.

Strawson, John. *Italian Campaign*, London, 1987.

Van Creveld, Martin. *Hitler's Strategy: The Balkan Clue*, Cambridge, 1973.

Vella, Philip. *Malta: Blitzed but not Beaten*, Valletta, 1989.

Warner, Geoffrey. *Iraq and Syria, 1941*, London, 1974.

Watson, Bruce Allen. *Exit Rommel: The Tunisian Campaign, 1942–1943*, Westport, 1999.

Wilson, Henry Maitland. *Eight Years Overseas, 1939–1947*, London, 1950.

Woodman, Richard. *Malta Convoys, 1940–1943*, London, 2000.

Wynter, H. W. *Special Forces in the Desert War, 1940–1943*, London, 2002.

Young, Desmond. *Rommel*, London, 1950.

Zweig, Ronald W. *Britain and Palestine During the Second World War*, Suffolk, 1986.

# Index

Addis Ababa 8, 30
Alam Halfa, battle of 9, 46
Albania 11, 22-24
Alexander, Harold, General 46, 51, 53, 57, 58, 78
Alexandria 6, 8, 14, 21, 25, 29, 36, 38, 41, 45, 86
Algeria 7, 14, 21, 22, 48, 54, 81, 82-83
Anglo-Egyptian Treaty 14
antitank guns 36-37
Anzio 9, 56-57
Aosta, Duke of 8, 10, 15, 29
*Ark Royal*, HMS 38, 39
Arnim, Jürgen von, General 18, 50-51
Athens 9
Auchinleck, Claude, General 37, 41, 42, 43, 45-46
Austria 9, 11, 66
Axis, Rome–Berlin 11-14, 18

Badoglio, Pietro, Marshal 54
Baghdad 8, 38, 84
Bagnold, Ralph, Captain 27
Balkans 11, 13, 66, 77-78
Bardia 28, 29
*Barham*, HMS 39
Bastico, Ettore, General 15, 18
Beda Fomm, battle of 8, 29
Belgrade 9, 31, 78
Benghazi 8, 29, 42, 48
   "Benghazi Handicap" 7
Bergonzoli, General 29
Blaskowitz, Johannes, General 58
*Bretagne* (French battleship) 25
British and Commonwealth troops 8, 19, 21, 27, 30, 34, 38, 50, 51, 57
   Eighth Army 7, 8, 9, 19, 21, 37, 42, 45, 46, 47, 51, 53, 54, 55, 56, 57, 78
   *see also* military strength, Britain; Upham VC and Bar, Charles Hazlitt
Bulgaria 77

Calabria 9, 25
Capuzzo, Fort 8
Cassino, Monte 9, 56, 57
casualties *see* losses
Cavagnari, Domenico, Admiral 17, 26
Cavallero, Count Ugo, Marshal 18, 41
*Cavour* (Italian battleship) 26
Churchill, Winston 11, 21, 24, 25, 27, 29, 31, 36, 37, 43, 46, 48-49, 53, 54, 56-57, 64, 65, 66, 68, 77-78
Clark, Mark, General 49-50, 54, 57-58
Crete
   airborne invasion of 8, 34-35
Cunningham, Alan, Lieutenant-General 30, 37, 42
Cunningham, Sir Andrew, Admiral 25, 41
Cyrenaica 8, 29, 31, 35
Czechoslovakia 11

Darlan, Admiral 38, 50
Dentz, Henri, General 8, 21, 38

Dodecanese Islands 10, 54, 66
*Duillo* (Italian battleship) 26
Duisberg (Axis batteship) 39
Dulles, Allan 79
*Dunquerque* (French battleship) 24, 25

*Eagle*, HMS 9, 47
Eden, Anthony 5, 31, 77-78
Egypt 7, 14, 22, 27-29, 45, 84-86
Eisenhower, Dwight, General 21, 49, 56, 65, 66, 70
El Agheila 7, 35, 48
El Alamein 7, 21, 45, 80
   first battle of 9, 45, 47
   second battle of 9, 47-48
Enigma machines *see* Ultra
Eritrea 8, 10, 82
Estéva, Admiral 50
Ethiopia 5, 8, 10, 82
executions 70, 72

Faisal II, King 84
Farouk, King 84, 86
Fascist Grand Council 9, 54
Florence 9
France 82-84
   Allied invasion of 58
   *see also* military strength, Vichy France
Franco, Francisco, General 13-14
Fredendall, Lloyd R., Major-General 49
Freyberg, Bernard, Lieutenant-General 34, 68
Friendship, Treaty of 13
*Furious*, HMS 38

Gambin, Leon 73-76
Gaule, Charles de 21, 38, 83
Gensoul, Marcel-Bruno, Admiral 24, 25
George Cross 8, 76
German troops 29, 34, 39, 41, 55, 56, 57, 58
   *Deutsches Afrika Korps* (DAK, later *Panzerarmee Afrika*) 7, 8, 9, 18, 29, 41, 43, 47, 48, 51
   *see also* military strength, Germany (including Axis)
Gibraltar 6, 13, 14, 21, 25, 38, 39, 47
Godfroy, René, Admiral 25
Graziani, Rodolfo, Marshal 8, 10, 15, 22, 27-28, 29, 51
Greece 8, 9, 22-24, 31, 34, 77-78
   resistance 71-72
Gustav line 56, 57

Habbaniyah 8, 37
Halder, General 36
Himmler, Heinrich 79
Hitler, Adolf 5, 7, 11, 12, 13, 14, 18, 22, 24, 26, 29, 31, 34, 35, 38, 39, 45, 53, 54, 55, 66, 67, 70, 86
Hube, Hans, General 54
Hungary 78, 78

*Illustrious*, HMS 26
Iran 7, 48, 84

Iraq  7, 14, 19, 37-38, 84
Italian Air Force  16-17
Italian Army  15, 19, 24, 27, 51
Italian East Africa  10
Italian Navy  17-18, 25-26
Italian troops  15-18, 24, 27, 41
Italy  54-58, 78-79, 81-82

*Kandahar*, HMS  41
Kassala  8
Kasserine Pass, battle of  9, 51
Kesselring, Albert, Field-Marshal  18, 19, 41, 45, 47, 55, 56, 57, 67

Lampson, Sir Miles  84
League of Nations  5, 10-11, 14
Lebanon  14, 38, 84
Leese, Oliver, General  56
*Littorio* (Italian battleship)  26
losses  25, 27, 28, 29, 30, 31, 35, 37, 38, 41, 42, 43, 47, 48, 50, 54, 56, 78, 80
Lucas, John, Major-General  56, 57
Lybia  81

Macedonia  9
Mackensen, Eberhard von, General  57
Malta  7, 8, 9, 14, 15, 25, 29
    siege of  21, 36, 38-39, 41, 45, 47, 73-76
Matapan, Cape, battle of  8, 31
medals
    George Cross  8, 76
    Victoria Cross  59, 61, 63
Mers-el-Kebir  8, 24-25
Messe, Giovanni, General  15
Messina  9, 54
Metaxas, Ioannis  31
Mihailoví, Dráa, General  70, 71
military strength
    Britain  19-21, 24, 25, 27, 41, 44, 47, 80
    Germany (including Axis)  41, 43, 77, 80
    Italy  15-18, 24, 27
    USA  21
    Vichy France  21, 24, 49
Montgomery, Bernard, General  19-21, 46, 47-48, 51, 53, 54, 56, 70
Morocco  14, 21, 22, 48, 83
Mussolini, Benito  5, 6, 8, 9, 10-13, 15, 22, 24, 26, 29, 41, 45, 52, 54, 66, 67, 79

Naples  9, 55
Neame, General  36
*Nelson*, HMS  17
*Neptune*, HMS  41

O'Connor, Richard, General  27, 35
*Ohio*, HMS  47
operations
    Anvil (Dragoon)  58
    Avalanche  9, 54-55
    Battleaxe  9, 36
    Baytown  9
    Brevity  8, 36
    Catapult  8, 24-25
    Compass  8, 28-29
    Crusader  8, 41
    Explorer  8, 38
    Halberd  39
    Hercules  45
    Husky  9, 53
    Lightfoot  9, 47
    Manna  9
    Marita  8, 31
    Merkur  8, 34-35
    Overlord  56, 58, 65, 66, 80
    Pedestal  47
    Shingle  9, 56
    Substance  39
    Supercharge  48
    Torch  9, 48-49
    Venezia  8

Pact of Steel  8, 12, 13
Palestine  7, 8, 14, 19, 37, 38, 86
Papagos, Alexandros, General  22-24, 31
Papandreou, George  77
Patch, Alexander, Lieutenant-General  58
Patton, George, General  21, 49, 53, 54, 58
Paul, Prince Regent, Yugoslavia  31
Peniakoff, Vladimir  27
Petacci, Clara  79
Pétain, Marshal  21, 50
Platt, William, General  30
Plöesti oil fields  31, 77
*Provence* (French battleship)  25

*Queen Elizabeth*, HMS  8, 41

Rashid Ali el-Gaylani  8, 37, 84
Red Army  9, 71, 72, 78
resistance
    Greece  71-72
    Yugoslavia  70-71, 72
Riccardi, Arturo, Admiral  26
*Richelieu* (French battleship)  25
Ritchie, Neil, Major-General  42, 45
*Roma* (Italian battleship)  54
Rome  9, 10, 54, 55, 56, 58, 66
Rommel, Erwin, Field-Marshal  7, 8, 18, 29, 35-37, 38, 39, 41-42, 43, 45-46, 50-51, 67, 70
Roosevelt, Franklin  7, 12, 21, 30, 48-49, 53, 54, 64, 65

Salerno  9, 54, 56
Scobie, Ronald, Lieutenant-General  77
Selassie, Haile  8, 10, 30
Sicily  9, 53-54
Sidi Barrani  8, 22, 28
Simovic, General  31
Sirte
    first battle of  8
    second battle of  8
Skorzeny, Otto  54
Sollum  8, 35
Somaliland, Italian  10, 30, 82
    British  29-30
Somerville, Sir James, Vice-Admiral  25
Spanish Civil War  6, 13
Stalin, Joseph  9, 77
Stirling, David, Lieutenant-Colonel  27
*Strasbourg* (French battleship)  24, 25
Sudan  8, 14, 19, 28, 29, 86
Suez Canal  5-6, 14, 86
supplies  38-39, 42-43, 46, 47
Syria  8, 14, 19, 21, 37-38, 83-84

tanks  28, 29, 37, 43
Taranto  8, 25-26
Tito (Josip Bró)  9, 71
Tobruk  8, 9, 29, 35-36, 41-42
    siege of  8, 42, 43, 48
Trieste  9, 77, 78, 79
Tripartite Pact  8, 31
Tripoli  9, 29, 48
Truscott, Lucius, General  57, 58
Tunisia  9, 14, 18, 21, 22, 50-51, 80, 83

Udine  9
Ultra  30, 35, 38, 67-70
Upham VC and Bar, Charles Hazlitt  59-63
Upham, Mary (Molly) Eileen  59, 63
US troops
    Fifth Army  9, 53, 54, 55, 56, 57, 58, 78-79
    Seventh Army  58
    Third Army  58
USA  21, 48-49

*Valiant*, HMS  8, 41
Vian, Philip, Vice-Admiral  38
Victor Emmanuelle, King  54
Victoria Cross  59, 61, 63
*Victorious*, HMS  38

Vietinghoff, Heinrich von, General  55, 78, 79
*Vittorio Veneto* (Italian battleship)  31

Wavell, Sir Archibald, General  19, 35, 36, 37
Weichs, Maximilian von, Field-Marshal  77
Weygand, General  21

Wilson, Maitland, Field-Marshal  21, 34, 38
Wingate, Orde, Lieutenant-Colonel  30
Wolff, Karl, General  79

Yugoslavia  9, 31-34, 77, 78
    resistance  70-71, 72

# About the Authors

Professor Robert O'Neill is the series editor of the Essential Histories. His wealth of knowledge and expertise shapes the series content and provides up-to-the-minute research and theory. Born in 1936 an Australian citizen, he served in the Australian army (1955–68) and has held a number of eminent positions in history circles, including the Chichele Professorship of the History of War at All Souls College, University of Oxford, 1987–2001, and the Chairmanship of the Board of the Imperial War Museum and the Council of the International Institute for Strategic Studies, London, England. He is the author of many books, including works on the German army and the Nazi party, and the Korean and Vietnam wars. Now based in Australia on his retirement from Oxford, he is the Chairman of the Council of the Australian Strategic Policy Institute.

Paul Collier has lived and worked extensively in England and Australia, where he completed his first degree at Adelaide University. He received his Doctor of Philosophy from the University of Oxford.